CREATING
a Winning Online
EXHIBITION

A Guide for Libraries, Archives, and Museums

MARTIN R. KALFATOVIC

AMERICAN LIBRARY ASSOCIATION
Chicago and London
2002

Cover and text design by Dianne M. Rooney

Cover: A Hundred Highlights (http://www.kb/nl/kb/100hoogte/hh-en.html) from the home page of Koninklijke Bibliotheek—National Library of the Netherlands (http://www.kb.nl). Used with permission

Composition by ALA Editions in Berkeley and Formata Regular typefaces using QuarkXpress 4.0 on a PC platform

Printed on 50-pound white offset, a pH-neutral stock, and bound in 10-point cover stock by McNaughton & Gunn

The paper used in this publication meets the minimum requirements of American National Standard for Information Sciences—Permanence of Paper for Printed Library Materials, ANSI Z39.48-1992. ⊚

ISBN: 0-8389-0817-9

Printed in the United States of America

06 05 04 03 02   5 4 3 2 1

FOR TERRY, 1927–2001

CONTENTS

ILLUSTRATIONS   *vii*

FOREWORD BY S. DIANE SHAW   *ix*

ACKNOWLEDGMENTS   *xi*

INTRODUCTION   *xiii*

1 Online Exhibitions versus Digital Collections   *1*

2 The Idea   *9*

3 Executing the Exhibition Idea   *20*

4 The Staff   *39*

5 Technical Issues: Digitizing   *44*

6 Technical Issues: Markup Languages   *54*

7 Technical Issues: Programming, Scripting, Databases, and Accessibility   *63*

8 Design   *72*

9 Online Exhibitions: Case Studies and Awards   *88*

10 Conclusion: Online with the Show!   *96*

APPENDIXES

A Sample Online Exhibition Proposal   *98*

B Sample Exhibition Script   *100*

C Guidelines for Reproducing Works from Exhibition Websites   *103*

D Suggested Database Structure for Online Exhibitions   *105*

E Timeline for Contracted Online Exhibitions   *107*

F Dublin Core Metadata of an Online Exhibition   *108*

G The Katharine Kyes Leab and Daniel J. Leab *American Book Prices Current* Exhibition Awards   *109*

H Bibliography of Exhibitions (Gallery and Virtual)   *111*

INDEX   *115*

ILLUSTRATIONS

CHAPTER 1 **Online Exhibitions versus Digital Collections**

    FIGURE 1   *Duane Hanson: An Exhibition*, Broward County Libraries Division, Bienes Center for the Literary Arts   4

    FIGURE 2   *Powers of Persuasion*, United States National Archives and Records Administration   5

CHAPTER 2 **The Idea**

    FIGURE 3   *From Smithson to Smithsonian*, Smithsonian Institution Libraries   10

    FIGURE 4   *Canada at Scale: Maps of Our History*, National Archives of Canada / Archives nationales du Canada   12

    FIGURE 5   *The Night before Christmas by Clement C. Moore, Illustrated*, Brown University Library   13

    FIGURE 6   *American Treasures of the Library of Congress*, Library of Congress   14

    FIGURE 7   *Dino at the Sands*, UNLV Libraries Special Collections   16

CHAPTER 3 **Executing the Exhibition Idea**

    FIGURE 8   *Science and the Artist's Book*, Smithsonian Institution Libraries   25

    FIGURE 9   *Nos Los Inquisidores*, Department of Special Collections of the University Libraries of Notre Dame   25

    FIGURE 10   *Frontier Photographer: Edward S. Curtis*, Smithsonian Institution Libraries   26

    FIGURE 11   *Jewish marriage contract, Nice, 1690*, Yale University Library Judaica Collection   28

    FIGURE 12   World's Fair literature from *"Make the Dirt Fly!"* Smithsonian Institution Libraries   31

    FIGURE 13   Bill hopper from *From Smithson to Smithsonian*, Smithsonian Institution Libraries   32

CHAPTER 8 **Design**

    FIGURE 14   Screen shot, Internet Explorer (version 5.0)   76

    FIGURE 15   Screen shot, Internet Explorer (version 5.0), full-screen mode   76

    FIGURE 16   Screen shot, Netscape Navigator (version 4.7)   77

CHAPTER 9   **Online Exhibitions: Case Studies and Awards**

FIGURE 17   *Bibliotheca Canadiana. A Historical Survey of Canadian Bibliography / Étude Historique de la Bibliographie Canadienne,* Rare Books and Special Collections Division, McGill University Libraries   *89*

FIGURE 18   *Halifax and Its People / 1749–1999,* Nova Scotia Archives and Records Management   *90*

FIGURE 19   *Do You Remember, When,* United States Holocaust Memorial Museum   *91*

FIGURE 20   *Nabokov under Glass: A Centennial Exhibition,* Henry W. and Albert A. Berg Collection of English and American Literature, Humanities and Social Sciences Library, New York Public Library   *93*

FOREWORD

With the introduction of the World Wide Web into everyday use across the globe, an immense potential audience, growing every day, exists for new collections-based Internet resources, such as online exhibitions. The Internet has brought great promise, as well as high expectations, for the roles that libraries and archives can play in supplementing educational programs and in fostering greater public access to the historical and cultural materials and records that they hold in their custody. Although libraries and archives may no longer think of online exhibitions as a particularly new method for reaching a worldwide audience interested in their collections, the task of creating effective online exhibitions that viewers will learn from, linger in, and enjoy remains a true challenge.

What makes a successful online exhibition? And how can library and archival staff members charged with doing online exhibitions be reasonably assured that the significant amount of time and effort they have to devote to such projects is well spent? Until now, there has been surprisingly little guidance directed specifically to the library and archival communities on how to go about doing online exhibitions. While it can be instructive to look at the many online exhibitions already available on the World Wide Web, browsing the almost infinite approaches and design choices can be confusing and intimidating, particularly for staff members with little experience in creating web pages or for those who want to try new things but aren't sure where to start. Doing online exhibitions can certainly be a flirtation with unexpected problems and uncertain results, but with luck, organization, good design sense, and experienced technical help, libraries and archives have a better chance of pulling off a show that everyone involved in can be proud of.

Fortunately, the book before you serves as a knowledgeable and trustworthy guide through the thorny process of creating dynamic online exhibitions featuring library and archival materials. In this book, Martin R. Kalfatovic, Digital Projects Librarian for the Smithsonian Institution Libraries, who has spearheaded projects resulting in several excellent online exhibitions, shares his hard-won insights into the most effective ways of handling each stage of the process while still encouraging readers to develop their own styles and tailor their online exhibition projects in ways that best suit the needs of their own collections and institutions. Whether the reader is new to doing online exhibitions or already has some experience with the genre, this book will serve as a welcome guide for executing a carefully planned and informed approach to mastering all aspects of creating online exhibitions.

My own personal interest in online exhibitions springs from *Science and the Artist's Book* (see figure 8, page 25), a gallery exhibition I co-curated in 1994 and 1995. This show was capably translated into an online exhibition for the Smithsonian Institution Libraries website in 1995. It is wonderful to have this online version of the show still available long after the gallery show has closed. Although the web version cannot replace the experience of standing in front of the exhibition cases and seeing the original artist's books and their accompanying landmark scientific texts, it is faithful to the spirit and style of the original gallery show, a quality that Martin, as the web designer, and my fellow curator Carol Barton and I strove together to achieve. It is gratifying to realize that more people are happening upon the online exhibition of *Science and the Artist's Book* every day. I know of at least two educators who have used the site to supplement their teaching and turn students on to artist's books—a development that could not have happened without the online version, especially since we never produced a printed catalog for the show.

Delighted as I am with the results of *Science and the Artist's Book* in its online form, I hope more libraries and archives will feel encouraged to start their own online exhibitions program, or to continue their existing program with renewed enthusiasm, with the help of this book. The author's observations and advice, grounded in years of experience designing online exhibitions, should certainly help make the process an easier one.

S. Diane Shaw
Smithsonian Institution Libraries

ACKNOWLEDGMENTS

Exhibitions are teamwork and I like to think of the following people as part of the team that brought this book on exhibitions to completion. Working at the Smithsonian Institution has many benefits and a few drawbacks. Among the drawbacks is the constant high quality of exhibitions (both online and gallery) constantly surrounding you. The leadership at Smithsonian Institution Libraries, however, has encouraged working to the highest level of quality possible. Director Nancy E. Gwinn, Assistant Directors Thomas Garnett and Mary Augusta Thomas, and former Assistant Director Bonita Perry (as well as former Director Barbara J. Smith) have provided regular support for the Libraries' ongoing online exhibition program.

At ALA Editions, editors Patrick Hogan and Tarshel Beards helped formulate my ideas and waited patiently for me to put them on paper. Cynthia Fostle and Karen Young were great helps in creating the final version of this book. An additional nod of thanks goes to Eric Bryant, my editor at *Library Journal,* for proposing an article on online exhibitions that helped to develop certain themes in the book.

For the online exhibitions that I have worked on, I owe a great debt to the various curators. These include William Baxter, Mary Augusta Thomas, Nancy E. Gwinn (Smithsonian Institution Libraries), and Bernard Finn (National Museum of American History, Smithsonian Institution). S. Diane Shaw, who also co-curated *Science and the Artist's Book,* also deserves special mention and thanks as the compiler of *Library and Archival Exhibitions on the Web* (available at: http://www.sil.si.edu/SILPublications/Online-Exhibitions), without which a work such as this would have been much more difficult. I will tentatively thank Courtney S. Danforth for teaching me everything I know about PhotoShop, Macs, and cheese grits.

Thanks also to Nancy L. Matthews, formerly of the Publications Office at Smithsonian Institution Libraries (and a million other things!), my second pair of eyes for nearly eight years of online publications, and to my wife, Mary, for putting up with too many long weekends of work! And lastly, thanks to Suzanne C. Pilsk for nudging this book to completion and for reading the final manuscript (giving much sound advice, some of which was actually heeded)!

INTRODUCTION

For the last twenty years, neither matter nor space nor time has been what it was from time immemorial. We must expect great innovations to transform the entire technique of the arts, thereby affecting artistic invention itself and perhaps even bringing about an amazing change in our very notion of art.—Paul Valéry

What appeared to French poet and essayist Paul Valéry as amazing innovations in the technology of art are now commonplace to those of us comfortable with television, motion pictures, and the multimedia world delivered to our computers through the Internet.

Libraries, archives, and museums are the great treasure houses of the human condition. These memory institutions, storing for future generations and, we hope, the ages, the information, knowledge, wisdom, artifacts, techniques, treasures, and examples of human endeavor, have evolved over the course of time, and many of their products and services of today would be unfamiliar to a visitor stumbling through their doors from as recently as a hundred years ago.

Historically, the three great repositories of human memory and the world, natural as well as created, have relied upon their generally unchallenged status as cultural institutions to disseminate their message. People came to libraries, archives, and museums to learn, to explore, and to be entertained. With the advent of electronic media—first radio, then television, and now the Internet—the traditional activities of learning, exploring, and entertainment moved from public arenas, such as libraries, archives, and museums, to living rooms and desktops.

Before looking specifically at how the Internet, through the medium of online exhibitions, can enhance the traditional roles of libraries and archives, let's take a quick look at exactly how these institutions can be defined.

MUSEUMS

The word *museum* comes from the Greek *mouseion*, a place of contemplation, a temple of the Muses. For the Romans, the museum was a place of philosophical discussion. Samuel Johnson (1755) defined the museum in his dictionary as a "Repository of learned Curiosities." Caspar F. Neickel (1727) of Hamburg, in his *Museographia*, termed it a "chamber of treasures—rarities—objects of nature—of art and of reason."

Historically, the term *museum* was first used in reference to the collection of Lorenzo the Magnificent (Florence, 1449 to 1492). More commonly used terms, generally from the sixteenth century, include *gallery* and *cabinet* (in both

English and French). In German, the terms *Kabinett* and *Kammer* were used, usually prefaced with a modifying term to describe more precisely the contents of the institution, for example, *Kunstkammer* (art cabinet), *Naturalienkabinett* (natural history cabinet), or *Wunderkammer* (curiosity cabinet; Lewis 1987, 10).

A more current definition of museum, from the American Association of Museums, says that to be described as a museum, an institution must meet the following criteria:

> Be a legally organized not-for-profit institution or part of a not-for-profit institution or government entity; be essentially educational in nature; have a formally stated mission; with one full-time paid professional staff person who has museum knowledge and experience, and is delegated authority and allocated financial resources sufficient to operate the museum effectively; present regularly scheduled programs and exhibits that use and interpret objects for the public according to accepted standards; have a formal and appropriate program of documentation, care, and use of collections and/or tangible objects; have a formal and appropriate program of maintenance and presentation of exhibits.

The International Council of Museums (ICOM) provides a similar definition:

> Non-profit-making, permanent institution in the service of society and of its development, and open to the public, which acquires, conserves, researches, communicates, and exhibits, for the purposes of study, education, and enjoyment, material evidence of man and his environment.

Though museums serve a multitude of audiences with a wide variety of programs, including films, lectures, and tours, the most familiar, as well as the most common, is the exhibition. Museum exhibitions may range from large-scale displays of hundreds of objects that remain on view for years (permanent exhibitions), to large but temporary exhibitions, to simple presentations of a few objects in a case in a lobby or hall.

LIBRARIES AND ARCHIVES

The American Library Association (1988) defines a library as

> An institution or agency, under the charge of a professional staff, which collects, organizes, preserves, and makes accessible books, periodicals, audiovisual materials, and other information-bearing media for the purposes of instruction, research, reference, or recreation of its clientele.

Similarly, the Society of American Archivists (Evans 1974, 417) defines an archive as

> (1) The noncurrent records of an organization or institution preserved because of their continuing value; also referred to, in this sense, as archival materials or archival holdings. (2) The agency responsible for selecting, preserving and making available archival materials.

At first glance, the similarities between museums, archives, and libraries may not be apparent. In some instances, the similarities are obvious. A number of libraries, including the Newberry Library, the Folger Shakespeare Library, the Huntington Library, and the Morgan Library, collect primarily rare materials and have major exhibition spaces. Archives may also maintain large exhibition areas or major displays, as does the National Archives and Records Administration for its presentation of the United States Constitution and the Declaration of Independence.

Libraries have a long history of using the exhibition of materials to promote their collections and the circulation of the materials on display. The Enoch Pratt Free Library in Baltimore, Maryland, has had an active program of exhibits that began in 1927 (Coplan 1974, 2). Promotional exhibits, which are in many respects closer to an advertising billboard than to a true narrative exhibition, do share some similarities to more museumlike exhibitions. Libraries that have become adept at them can transfer the lessons they have learned to the creation of narrative exhibitions.

In a narrative exhibition, which may not directly encourage the circulation of materials (indeed, the focus of a narrative exhibition will be rare or special collections that do not circulate), even the smallest of libraries and archives can create a display to promote their institutions and give their public a wider view of their collections. Now, with the advent of the Internet and the ability to create online exhibitions, the constraints of space and time (and to some extent money) no longer hinder libraries and archives in the creation of exhibitions that will accomplish the same goals on an even grander scale.

ONLINE EXHIBITIONS

In his article "The Neon Paintbrush," Peter Walsh (2000, 48) tells us that exhibitions presented on the Web "will not just present important images in a new technology. That technology will almost certainly change how those images are seen and what they mean." If Walsh is correct, we must be careful as we take our traditional gallery-bound conception of the library and archival exhibition and transform it for presentation on the Web.

And yet, even with this caveat in mind, online exhibitions from museums, libraries, and archives hit the Internet early. The Library of Congress, for example, made the text files and images from exhibitions such as *1492: An Ongoing Voyage, Scrolls from the Dead Sea: The Ancient Library of Qumran and Modern Scholarship,* and *Revelations from the Russian Archives* available on a file transfer protocol (FTP) site in 1992 and 1993. These early efforts provided little interactivity and simply allowed the user to download portions of the exhibition—in the case of the *Revelations from the Russian Archives,* for instance, transcriptions of documents and selected images, with no real organization. By 1996, however, the tremendous growth of the World Wide Web as the primary method of the public's interaction with the Internet saw an explosion in the presentation of online exhibitions by museums, libraries, and archives.

Now, online exhibitions are a regular offering from our cultural institutions. Online exhibitions have also become an almost necessary adjunct to traditional physical exhibitions, offering a continuing life to the ideas presented in the brick-and-mortar galleries long after the exhibitions have closed. Additionally, we are seeing an increasing number of virtual-only exhibitions in which museums, libraries, and archives are using the traditional notions of the exhibition as springboards to create interesting, instructive, and fun exhibitions that will never see visitors walking through them. The benefits of online exhibitions are many and include the abilities to showcase objects that could never be on view in a gallery space due to their fragility or value, to present (for libraries and archives, especially) numerous page openings or leaves of manuscripts, and to create exhibitions that are, generally, far less expensive than gallery exhibitions.

As we move to provide increased access to our collections in the form of online exhibitions, it is important to remember why we are creating exhibitions in the first place. The purpose of the exhibition in a museum is generally quite clear. The museum, to a great extent, exists to serve the exhibition. In libraries and archives, however, an exhibition, whether real or virtual, is an adjunct to a host of other missions and services. In most cases, the exhibition in a library or archive will enhance other programs.

Additionally, as museums have learned, their real treasures are their objects. The picture of an object on a computer monitor does not have the same level of reality, the same gravitas, as the physical object itself has in front of a visitor's eyes. The goodwill and publicity that gallery exhibitions can generate when visitors are allowed to interact with the collections of a library or archive should not be underestimated. And just as museums need to deal with this issue when creating online exhibitions, so do libraries and archives. The nature of objects in libraries and archives, however, lends those objects to online presentation. Though books and documents are inherently three-dimensional and suffer from the same loss of depth that museum objects do, the value of the library and archival materials often lies between the covers, in the two-dimensional space of the page. Unlike a physical exhibition, which allows only one view of an object, an online exhibition permits the presentation of numerous page openings or pages of a document.

At the same time, libraries and archives must be careful to resist the temptation simply to put up a number of pretty pictures and call it an exhibition. In the chapters that follow, we will trace the steps required to create a successful exhibition of library and archival materials, from finding the idea to assembling the staff to coping with the technical and aesthetic issues that determine the quality of the product that the public ultimately sees.

SOURCES CITED

American Association of Museums. "Museum Accreditation: Criteria and Characteristics." Available at: http://www.aam-us.org/webc&c.htm.

American Library Association. 1988. *ALA Handbook of Organization.* Chicago: ALA.

Coplan, Kate. 1974. *Effective Library Exhibits.* Dobbs Ferry, W.Va.: Oceana.

Evans, Frank B., Donald F. Harrison, and Edwin A. Thompson. 1974. "A Basic Glossary for Archivists, Manuscript Curators, and Records Managers." Ed. William L. Rofes. *American Archivist* 37, no. 3 (July): 417.

International Council of Museums. "ICOM Code of Professional Ethics." Available at: http://www.icom.org/ethics.htm.

Lewis, Geoffrey D. 1987. "Collections, Collectors and Museums: A Brief World Survey." In *Manual of Curatorship,* ed. John M. A. Thompson et al. London: Butterworths.

Rare Book and Manuscript Section. ACRL. "Library Web Exhibitions." Available at: http://www.library.yale.edu/~mtheroux/webecac.htm.

Valéry, Paul. 1964. "The Conquest of Ubiquity." In *Aesthetics,* trans. Ralph Manheim. New York: Pantheon. Quoted in Walter Benjamin, "The Work of Art in the Age of Mechanical Reproduction," *Illuminations* (New York: Schocken, 1969), 217–251.

Walsh, Peter. 2000. "The Neon Paintbrush: Seeing, Technology, and the Museum as Metaphor." *Journal of the American Society for Information Science* 51, no. 1: 39–48.

ONLINE EXHIBITIONS DISCUSSED

1492: An Ongoing Voyage. Library of Congress.
http://lcweb.loc.gov/exhibits/1492/intro.html

Revelations from the Russian Archives. Library of Congress.
http://www.loc.gov/exhibits/archives/intro.html

Scrolls from the Dead Sea: The Ancient Library of Qumran and Modern Scholarship. Library of Congress.
http://www.loc.gov/exhibits/scrolls/toc.html

CHAPTER

1

Online Exhibitions versus Digital Collections

What is an online exhibition? Is a collection of objects on the Web an exhibition? What about digital collections? Can they be an online exhibition?

COLLECTION OR EXHIBITION?

It is very important to remember that a collection of objects does not make an exhibition. It is only when objects are carefully chosen to illustrate a theme and tied together by a narrative or other relational threads that they become an exhibition. The Web has enabled museums, libraries, and archives, as never before, to present their collections to a wider public. With the explosion in the growth of the Web since the mid-1990s, the availability of collections from these institutions has been expanding exponentially.

However, pinning down just what a digital collection is or how to define it has been a problem since memory institutions (museums, libraries, and archives) began to create them. Patricia A. McClung, in her 1996 *Digital Collections Inventory Report,* noted that

> There are innumerable projects which feature pictorial images (e.g., photograph collections, maps, drawings of some sort, or museum collections); there are documentary text editing projects for individual personal papers; there are literary and historical text encoding projects (which for the most part feature SGML encoding); there are efforts to convert entire collections or to provide a critical mass of materials in a particular subject area; and there are a wide variety of experimental projects of one flavor or another. In addition to projects which convert print-based and/or photographic materials, there are a host of mixed-media projects, as well as projects focused on additional formats such as sound recordings, films, microfilm, motion picture film, etc. There are also a number of initiatives to make materials whose original format is electronic widely available via the Internet.

To get a better idea of how the mounting of collections on the Web differs from an actual online exhibition, let's look at a few types of online collections from museums, libraries, and archives.

Museum Collections on the World Wide Web

The National Portrait Gallery of the Smithsonian Institution maintains a database of approximately ten thousand records that represent holdings from its permanent and study collections. This database provides data about each object (accession number, title, sitter, artist, classification, materials, date, dimensions, current owner, acquisition) and, in many cases, a digital surrogate of the object.

Similarly, New York City's American Museum of Natural History has a project entitled "Amphibian Species of the World." This project contains a wealth of information about amphibian species, including an extensive bibliography.

Other examples can be found on sites by the National Warplane Museum in Illinois, which includes an online guide to warplanes, aircraft engines, and pilot interviews and stories; the Museum of Television and Radio, which has portions of its collections online; and the National Gallery of Art, which, like the National Portrait Gallery, has an advanced search interface to portions of its collections.

None of these, however, are exhibitions. They are merely collections online.

Archival Collections on the World Wide Web

Archives, too, offer countless collections online. The National Archives and Records Administration provides access to its holdings on the Web as well as documents relating to the census, genealogy, and other topics. The Archives of American Art at the Smithsonian Institution offers online access to records of its collections as well as a few selected documents. Similarly, many university and other specialized archives offer some type of access (online finding aids, database of archival records, full-text rekeyed or scanned documents) from their collections.

None of these, however, are exhibitions. They are merely collections online.

Library Collections on the World Wide Web

Libraries, through their online catalogs, have been providing some form of remote access to their collections since the early 1990s. If one includes data records in the large international bibliographic utilities such as the Research Library Group's Research Libraries Information Network (RLIN) and OCLC, Inc.'s World-Cat, online access to library collections can be dated to the early 1970s.

More recently, libraries have begun to make the full text of their collections available in an online environment. These digital collections can be large-scale efforts, such as the "Making of America" project from the University of Michigan and Cornell University, which is "a digital library of primary sources in American social history from the antebellum period through reconstruction." This collection contains over sixteen hundred books and fifty thousand journal articles. Similar projects include the Digital Scriptorium at Duke University, which is "both a physical and 'virtual' center in the Duke University Rare Book, Manuscript, and Special Collections Library, with offices in the Library and a Web site on the Internet," and the University of Virginia's Early American Fiction project, which will eventually contain the full text of 421 works by eighty-one authors.

Other projects are more narrowly focused. For example, the University of California, Berkeley, has among its many online offerings the Online Medieval and Classical Library, which includes such medieval texts as *The Anglo-Saxon Chronicle, The Story of the Ere-Dwellers (Eyrbyggja Saga), Orlando Furioso,* and John Gower's *Confessio Amantis.* And the Smithsonian Institution Libraries offers a number of rare natural history, history of science and technology, and anthropology texts online for both the researcher and the casual visitor. An example of a single work comes from Germany, where the Göttingen State and University Library (Niedersächsische Staats- und Universitätsbibliothek Göttingen) has placed a full-text image version of the Göttingen Gutenberg Bible (ca. 1454) online.

Again, however, none of these are exhibitions. They are merely collections online.

Though a collection may have an idea behind it (e.g., the "Making of America" project cited above), what separates an exhibition from a collection is that an exhibition has a tight connection between its idea, objects, and script that ties them all together. It is this tight connection that is vital; otherwise, a virtual exhibition will "amount to little more than disorganized and decontextualized digital collections" (Silver 1997, 826).

TYPES OF EXHIBITIONS

In what ways can this connection between idea, object, and script, so necessary and distinguishing to an online exhibition, be created and maintained? The obvious answer is that you start with a good idea and present the objects that carry through with the idea. Another way is to build themes. If your collections are strong in one particular area, build a whole exhibition around that collection. On the other hand, if you do not have enough objects for a particular theme, you might want to modify your idea by either broadening it or combining it with other ideas (e.g., if you don't have much material on Egypt, do a show on travel literature that will draw from other areas of strength).

In defining your idea, you will need to think about the different effects that you wish the exhibition to create. Though a good exhibition will elicit a range of emotions and reactions from its viewers, in most cases, an exhibition will aim for one particular effect. Five types of exhibition effects that you may wish to consider are

Aesthetic: organized around the beauty of the objects

Emotive: designed to illicit an emotion in the viewer

Evocative: designed to create an atmosphere

Didactic: constructed to teach about something specific

Entertaining: presented just for fun!

An *aesthetic exhibition* is one that exists purely for the sake of presenting beautiful objects. In the case of library and archival exhibitions, the purely aesthetic show may focus on rare materials or prints and photographs. *A Printmaker's Journey: The Graphic Art of Jorg Schmeisser* is a good example of an aesthetic exhibition created by Georgetown University's Lauinger Library. This exhibition, which in its gallery version showed forty-nine intaglio prints by Jörg Schmeisser, the German-born master printmaker and head of printmaking at the Australian National University in Canberra, displays nine of them in the online version. *The Sculpture of Donal Hord,* by the San Diego Historical Society, is an excellent example of an exhibition that primarily explores the aesthetic value of the works on display. Another example is *Duane Hanson: An Exhibition,* from Broward County Libraries (see figure 1). This exhibition moves beyond the purely aesthetic by including a number of supplemental items, such as models and tools used by the artist. And as a final example, *Season's Greetings: Holiday Cards from the Archives of American Art* presents a selection of holiday cards designed by artists from the 1920s through the 1980s.

Emotive exhibits exist primarily to elicit an emotion in the viewer. Many topics could easily fall into this category. *They Still Draw Pictures: Drawings Made by Spanish Children during the Spanish Civil War,* from the University of California, San Diego, Mandeville Special Collections Library, brings together over six hundred drawings made by children during the Spanish civil war. Originally printed in book form to raise money and support for relief efforts during the war, the online exhibition reproduces the original artworks, which continue to have the power to arouse deep emotions in the viewer. Likewise, the United States Holocaust Memorial Museum's *The Nazi Olympics: Berlin 1936,* an exhibition drawn from the museum's extensive archival holdings, evokes the nationalism and racism in Nazi Germany that led to the Holocaust. A last example, *Relief of Pain and Suffering,* from the University of California, Los Angeles, Louise M. Darling Biomedical Library's History and Special Collection, both traces the history of pain relief and draws the viewer into the world of pain itself.

FIGURE 1 | *Duane Hanson: An Exhibition.* Broward County Libraries Division, Bienes Center for the Literary Arts.

The purpose of an *evocative exhibition* is to create a specific atmosphere for the viewer. From the National Archives and Records Administration comes *Powers of Persuasion* (see figure 2). This exhibition, with its poster art from the Second World War (and even a war bonds audio file), attempts to bring the viewer into the anxious times that led to the creation of such posters.

Two other exhibitions, *Travel Photographs from the Collections of the Ohio Historical Society* and *Past Perfect: The Jewish Experience in Early-Twentieth-Century Postcards* (from the Library of the Jewish Theological Seminary), use, respectively, photographs and postcards to bring to life the past. As the curators of *Past Perfect* note in their introduction to the exhibition, "The colorful images that adorn these postcards afford a nostalgic view into a bygone world."

On a lighter note, *Sublime Anxiety: The Gothic Family and the Outsider* (from University of Virginia Library, Special Collections) uses an interesting and entertaining mix of graphics and web page layout to evoke the Gothic atmosphere. Included along with traditional examples of the Gothic, contemporary writer Anne Rice and artist Edward Gorey. Curator Natalie Regensburg explains that "the gothic in general, and this exhibition in particular, explores the tension between what we most fear and what we most desire. Its extraordinary popularity today, 200 years after the publication of the first gothic novel, shows us that the concern with freedom and connection is as relevant as it has ever been."

Though it is hoped that the viewer will learn something from an exhibition (be it virtual or gallery based), in some cases the exhibition will have a specific *didactic* focus. In a didactic exhibition, the curator aims to teach the viewer about a specific topic. An example of a didactic exhibition from the University of Arizona Library, Special Collections, is *Morris Udall: A Lifetime of Service to Arizona and the United States*. The creators of this exhibition state its purpose as to "present the papers and photographs of the Morris K. Udall Papers held by the University of Arizona Library Special Collections Department. The material in this exhibit will provide the user with an introduction to the collection as well as a sample of selected photographic images." In this example, a digital collection (the papers of Udall) are supplemented with an online exhibition that provides additional narrative context.

The Mount Holyoke College Archives and Special Collections exhibition *An Online Exhibit of Erotica* explores the "definition of erotica as that which is designed to cause arousal through suggestive rather than explicit portrayal of

FIGURE 2 | *Powers of Persuasion.* United States National Archives and Records Administration.

sexual acts." By focusing on printed works in the collections (erotica, the curators note, is not a specialty of the collections), the exhibition strives to define a relationship between printed and verbal erotica.

A final example, *Paper Dinosaurs, 1824–1969: An Exhibition of Original Publications from the Collections of the Linda Hall Library,* attempts to show how the depiction of dinosaurs in printed materials changed over the course of nearly 150 years. The curators describe how "in spite of the great popularity of dinosaurs, very few people have ever had the opportunity to see firsthand the original publications that revealed dinosaurs to the world. . . . Another problem with encountering the visual history of dinosaur discovery through secondary sources is that many quite significant images have never been reproduced at all."

Whether an exhibition's purpose is to teach or to be a purely aesthetic experience, in nearly every case there is a level of pure *entertainment.* In many ways, it is the element of entertainment that separates an exhibition from a textbook or a lecture.

Though football is, of course, more then mere entertainment to many, sports of all types can make for very entertaining online exhibitions. From the University of Notre Dame Archives comes *The Notre Dame v. USC Game: 22 October 1977.* This exhibition includes images, film footage, and sound clips of the game in which Notre Dame beat the favored USC Trojans on their way to a national championship.

In the way of pure entertainment, however, the Tufts University Archives has created an online exhibition, *Project Jumbo,* that will serve to forever dispel the notion that archivists and librarians have no sense of humor. The introductory text to the exhibition lays out the bold scope and nature of the exhibition:

> Since the devastating fire of 1975, Tufts has been without its mascot, Jumbo. All that remains of the once proud beast is his tail, carefully preserved in the University Archives. Now, with the miracle of modern technology, comes Project Jumbo, a bold plan to clone the original elephant, starting from his tail, and working upwards to the rest of his body. While most cloning projects attempt to create live animals, Project Jumbo is unique in its attempt to clone an actual stuffed elephant.

On a more literary note, the University Archives of Virginia Tech created *A Gallery of Bloomsday Cards,* an online exhibition of postcards created by T. E. Kennelly in honor of Bloomsday, June 16, the day in the life of Leopold Bloom that James Joyce chronicles in *Ulysses.*

Though an exhibition may have as its focus one of the methods noted above, most exhibitions will, in reality, combine elements from two or more of the types when it is created.

SOURCES CITED

McClung, Patricia A. 1996. *Digital Collections Inventory Report.* Council on Library Resources and Commission on Preservation and Access. Available at: http://www.clir.org/pubs/reports/mcclung/mccllong.html.

Silver, David. 1997. "Interfacing American Culture: The Perils and Potentials of Virtual Exhibitions." *American Quarterly* 49, no. 4: 825–850.

ONLINE EXHIBITIONS DISCUSSED

Duane Hanson: An Exhibition. Broward County Libraries Division, Bienes Center for the Literary Arts.
http://www.co.broward.fl.us/lii08200.htm

A Gallery of Bloomsday Cards. University Archives of Virginia Tech.
http://spec.lib.vt.edu/specgen/blooms/bloom.htm

Morris Udall: A Lifetime of Service to Arizona and the United States. University of Arizona Library, Special Collections.
http://dizzy.library.arizona.edu/branches/spc/udall/homepage.html

The Nazi Olympics: Berlin 1936. United States Holocaust Memorial Museum.
http://www.ushmm.org/olympics/index.html

The Notre Dame v. USC Game: 22 October 1977. University of Notre Dame Archives.
http://lamb.archives.nd.edu/77usc/77usc.html

An Online Exhibit of Erotica. Mount Holyoke College Archives and Special Collections.
http://www.mtholyoke.edu/lits/library/arch/exhibits/erotica.html

Paper Dinosaurs, 1824–1969: An Exhibition of Original Publications from the Collections of the Linda Hall Library. Linda Hall Library.
http://www.lhl.lib.mo.us/pubserv/hos/dino/welcome.htm

Past Perfect: The Jewish Experience in Early-Twentieth-Century Postcards. Library of the Jewish Theological Seminary.
http://www.jtsa.edu/library/exhib/pcard/index.shtml

Powers of Persuasion. United States National Archives and Records Administration.
http://www.nara.gov/exhall/powers/powers.html

A Printmaker's Journey: The Graphic Art of Jorg Schmeisser. Georgetown University, Lauinger Library.
http://www.library.georgetown.edu/dept/speccoll/schmeiss/schmeiss.htm

Project Jumbo. Tufts University Archives.
http://www.library.tufts.edu/archives/clone/pj.html

Relief of Pain and Suffering. University of California, Los Angeles, Louise M. Darling Biomedical Library's History and Special Collection.
http://www.library.ucla.edu/libraries/biomed/his/PainExhibit/index.html

The Sculpture of Donal Hord. San Diego Historical Society.
http://w ww.sandiegohistory.org/hord/hord.htm

Season's Greetings: Holiday Cards from the Archives of American Art. Archives of American Art, Smithsonian Institution.
http://artarchives.si.edu/exhibits/xmascard/xmascard.htm

Sublime Anxiety: The Gothic Family and the Outsider. University of Virginia Library, Special Collections.
  http://www.lib.virginia.edu/exhibits/gothic/open.html

They Still Draw Pictures: Drawings Made by Spanish Children during the Spanish Civil War. University of California, San Diego, Mandeville Special Collections Library.
  http://orpheus.ucsd.edu/speccoll/tsdp/index.html

Travel Photographs from the Collections of the Ohio Historical Society. Ohio Historical Society.
  http://www.ohiohistory.org/resource/audiovis/exhibit/travel/index.html

OTHER WEBSITES DISCUSSED

"Amphibian Species of the World." American Museum of Natural History.
  http://research.amnh.org/herpetology/amphibia/index.html

The Archives of American Art. Smithsonian Institution.
  http://artarchives.si.edu

The Digital Scriptorium. Duke University.
  http://scriptorium.lib.duke.edu/scriptorium

Early American Fiction project. University of Virginia.
  http://etext.lib.virginia.edu/eaf

The Göttingen Gutenberg Bible. Göttingen State and University Library.
  http://www.gutenbergdigital.de

"Making of America." University of Michigan and Cornell University.
  http://moa.umdl.umich.edu/ and http://moa.cit.cornell.edu

The Museum of Television and Radio.
  http://www.mtr.org

National Archives and Records Administration.
  http://www.nara.gov

National Gallery of Art.
  http://www.nga.gov/collection/collect.htm

National Portrait Gallery. Smithsonian Institution.
  http://portraits.npg.si.edu

The National Warplane Museum.
  http://www.warplane.org

Online Medieval and Classical Library. University of California, Berkeley.
  http://sunsite.berkeley.edu/OMACL

Smithsonian Institution Libraries.
  http://www.sil.si.edu

CHAPTER

2

The Idea

The best exhibitions, whether they exist in a gallery space or online, start with an idea. The idea, or concept, behind an exhibition is what will set it apart from a random collection of objects or, in the case of an online exhibition, images. An idea, well conceived, thoroughly thought through, properly executed, and carefully illustrated with objects, can provide the visitor not only with an educational experience, but also with an experience that will provoke further exploration of the topic. In the case of an online exhibition, this further exploration may be encouraged through the addition of supplemental materials or hyperlinks to other resources. Visitors to an online exhibition may also be intrigued enough to visit your collection or their own local collections that can assist them in their explorations.

WHERE TO GET IDEAS

According to Plato, an idea is a model or archetype of which things in the real world are but imperfect representations. Though in most cases, our exhibitions will never match the perfect conception we have of them in our mind's eye, the generation of exhibition ideas does not have to rely on shadows cast on the wall of a cave. The topics for an online exhibition are all around us and the materials to make those topics successful exhibitions are on our shelves.

A few general topics for which every library or archive can find materials around which to build an online exhibition include the following:

Anniversaries of births, deaths, or significant events in people's lives

Notable events in the life of an institution or region

Specific materials from certain collections or subcollections

Themes built around materials in the collection

Treasures

Work done by various departments of the library, archives, or other units or departments of the parent institution

Odd and unusual

Each of these areas can be tailored and focused to reflect the strengths of your individual library or archive. Examples of these themes, with comments on how they can be developed, are detailed below.

Anniversaries

Centennials, sesquicentennials, bicentennials, silver and golden anniversaries, diamond jubilees, or any other magic number that ends in a five or zero can be the impetus for an exhibition. An exhibition themed around an anniversary will allow you to revisit the past, highlight current collections or programs, and look forward to the next five, ten, one hundred years!

From Smithson to Smithsonian: The Birth of an Institution, an exhibition by Smithsonian Institution Libraries, is a prime example of an anniversary-themed exhibition. Created for the 150th anniversary of the founding of the Smithsonian Institution, *From Smithson to Smithsonian* traces the history of Englishman James Smithson's gift to the United States for the founding of an institution "for the increase and diffusion of knowledge" (see figure 3).

Near the end of the nineteenth century, the World's Columbian Exposition celebrated the four hundredth anniversary of Columbus's contact with the Americas. One hundred years later, the Library of Congress documented the

FIGURE 3 | *From Smithson to Smithsonian.* Courtesy Smithsonian Institution Libraries.

quincentenary of this event with *1492: An Ongoing Voyage.* An online version of this exhibition was later created that reflected much of the content of the gallery exhibition.

An exhibition from Ohio State University Archives, *1997: A Year of Many Anniversaries,* focuses not on a single anniversary but on the year 1997. In that year were anniversaries of nine separate events (ranging from the establishment of Benton County in 1847 to Professor Harold Evans's election to the National Academy of Sciences in 1972) that are documented through a photographic exhibition created from archival holdings.

Notable Events

Major events are perfect topics for online exhibitions. Libraries and archives often hold substantial materials related to significant, interesting, or even sometimes just entertaining events. An event-themed exhibition allows the library or archive to draw on a range of materials and in some cases collaborate with other institutions, such as historical societies, museums, or businesses.

The Chicago Fire, from the Chicago Historical Society, offers an overview of the great fire of 1871. The exhibition tells the story of the fire through photographs and an extensive collection of documents related to the fire, including testimony from Mrs. O'Leary (of cow fame).

Similarly, another event of historic importance, if less well known, is documented in *The Capture of Fort William and Mary, New Castle, New Hampshire, December 14–15, 1774,* from the University of New Hampshire, Milne Special Collections and Archives.

At the same time, very local events are also suitable for online exhibitions. The Public Library of New Orleans opened a new main library on December 15, 1958, at 219 Loyola Avenue. The exhibition *219 Loyola: Building a Library for New Orleans,* created by the New Orleans Public Library, explores the idea of building a new public library by examining (through the use of photographs, archival records, and printed materials) the planning for the new building, the construction, and the public and critical reaction to the structure.

Specific Materials

Special collections are the logical first place to turn when looking for an exhibition topic based on specific types of materials. Examples of special materials include such obvious ones as photographs, sheet music, and manuscripts, but may also include unique collections of postcards, bookbindings, and even postage stamps.

As an example of this last format, the Department of Rare Books and Special Collections, University Libraries of Notre Dame, has created an exhibition, *The Dr. Charles Wolf Collection of Irish Postage Stamps,* which centers on an Irish philatelic collection donated by Dr. Charles Wolf.

Maps and other cartographic materials provide a wealth of ideas for online exhibitions. *Canada at Scale: Maps of Our History* (National Archives of Canada / Archives nationales du Canada; see figure 4), *Exploring Africa: An Exhibit of Maps and Travel Narratives* (Thomas Cooper Library, University of South Carolina), *The Earth and the Heavens: The Art of the Mapmaker* (the British Library), *Highlights of the Map Collection, National Library of Scotland,* and *The Cartographic Creation of New England* (the Osher Map Library and Smith Center for Cartographic Education, University of Southern Maine) all use maps or cartography as their basic exhibition idea.

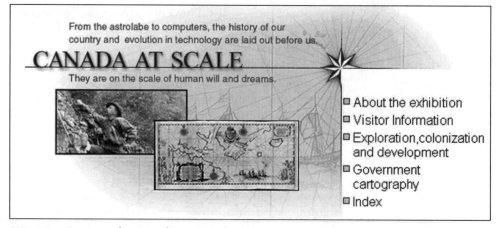

FIGURE 4 | *Canada at Scale: Maps of Our History.* National Archives of Canada / Archives nationales du Canada.

The range of special materials that appear in online exhibitions reflects the creativity of the exhibitions' creators. For example, postcards form the basis for *California Pacific Exposition: San Diego 1935–1936* (San Diego Historical Society); paper bindings are the focus of *The Enduring Legacy of Paper Bindings* (New York University's Bobst Library); and Soviet children's books take the spotlight in *Children's Books of the Early Soviet Era: Yesterday, Today and . . . Tomorrow* (Rare Books and Special Collections Division, McGill University Libraries).

Themes

Perhaps the most common exhibition idea is the themed exhibition. This type of exhibition will be built around a specific idea and designed to develop that idea. Themes can range from individuals to professions, poems, social movements or phenomena, collectors, and specific media.

Dr. Seuss Went to War: A Catalog of Political Cartoons by Dr. Seuss, from the Mandeville Special Collections Library, University of California, San Diego, is an example of a very specific theme: the wartime cartoons of Theodor Seuss Geisel. Arranged in chronological order, the cartoons show a side of Dr. Seuss that is not often seen. Similarly, *Churchill: The Evidence,* from the Churchill Archives Center, traces the life and times of Winston Churchill.

More examples of exhibitions that use as their idea a specific theme include *Connies* (State Library of Victoria, Australia), which celebrates Melbourne's tram conductors; *The Night before Christmas by Clement C. Moore, Illustrated* (Brown University Library; see figure 5), which uses an array of illustrations from the poem; and *Girls Fight for a Living* (created for Women's History Month by the University of Louisville Special Collections), which draws on a number of resources to examine the role of women in the workplace.

For an example of a medium used as the basis for an exhibition theme, one can look at *The History of Railway Photography* (Library Archive, The National Railway Museum, Great Britain). Because the exhibition relies exclusively on photographs to tell the story of British railways, its dual themes, railways and photographs, are focused and direct.

An Exhibition from the Collections of the John Hay Library

Brown University

FIGURE 5 | *The Night before Christmas by Clement C. Moore, Illustrated.* Brown University Library.

Treasures

A special subsection of the themed exhibition is the exhibition that highlights treasures of a collection. How different institutions will define just what part of their collections are their treasures varies greatly. The Library of Congress's *American Treasures of the Library of Congress* is an exhibition of documents such as Lincoln's first draft of the Gettysburg Address, Lafayette's copy of the Declaration of the Rights of Man, and Jefferson's draft of the Virginia Constitution (see figure 6). By any measure, these are unique treasures and ideal for online exhibitions. However, a wide range of materials can serve as the basis for treasure exhibitions. Other national and state libraries have mounted such exhibitions. A few additional examples include *Treasures of the Royal Library,* from the State Library of Denmark, and *Treasures from Europe's National Libraries,* from the Conference of European National Librarians.

The American Philosophical Society, in the exhibition *Treasures of the APS,* defines as treasures any items that stand out for the "extraordinary stories they tell about the history of this nation, the workings of science, or the culture in which we live." The Library of Virginia, in the exhibition *The Common Wealth: Treasures from the Collections of the Library of Virginia,* places "personal photographs, business records, and family histories that document the lives of all Virginians" in the treasure category. In a similar vein, *Treasures of Florida Libraries: A Celebration of Rare and Unique Materials,* from the University of Miami Library, brings together a host of materials from twenty-nine Florida libraries. On a much smaller scale is the University of Kansas Libraries' *Irish Treasures from the O'Hegarty Irish Collection*. This exhibition displays eighteen images from the libraries' Irish collection.

AMERICAN TREASURES ✴ OF THE ✴ LIBRARY OF CONGRESS

Treasure-Talks
List of Objects Currently on Exhibit
Funding and Credits

The Library of Congress gratefully acknowledges
the generous support of
The Document Company
XEROX
which has made possible the unprecedented
American Treasures exhibition and this online
presentation.

✴ EXHIBITION SECTIONS ✴
Exhibition Overview - Top Treasures
Memory - Reason - Imagination

Of the more than 121 million items in the Library of Congress, which are considered "treasures"? Of course Thomas Jefferson's handwritten draft of the Declaration of Independence is a treasure, not only because of its association with Jefferson but also because of what it reveals about how one of the founding documents of America was written and rewritten and finally agreed upon by dozens of men in the midst of a political crisis.

But what about Jelly Roll Morton's early compositions? Or Maya Lin's original drawing for the Vietnam Veterans Memorial? Or one of the earliest known baseball cards? Or the first motion picture deposited for copyright? The Library holds all these and more.

Thomas Jefferson, whose personal library became the core of the Library of Congress, arranged his books into three types of knowledge, corresponding to Francis Bacon's three faculties of the mind: Memory (History), Reason (Philosophy), and Imagination (Fine Arts).

Although the Library organizes its immense collections according to a system created at the end of the1800s, the treasures in this exhibition have been placed in the same categories that Jefferson would have used, had he been deciding where to put Alexander Graham Bell's lab notebook or George Gershwin's full orchestral score for *Porgy and Bess*.

Online Survey on Library of Congress Exhibitions
Exhibitions Home Page   Library of Congress Home Page

Library of Congress
Comments: *lcweb@loc.gov (January 17, 2001)*

FIGURE 6 | *American Treasures of the Library of Congress.* Library of Congress.

A much different approach to the treasures concept was taken by Texas A&M University's Cushing Library. In the exhibition *Fruits of a Research Collection,* the uses of a special collection for nontraditional research are highlighted. Steven E. Smith, Special Collections Librarian, noted that the "collections . . . have also been used by many . . . people for many other purposes—for example, journalists writing articles for national magazines, film producers creating documentaries, student groups making t-shirts, and book editors in search of cover art."

Work Done

An exhibition that focuses on the work done at the library or archive or at the parent institution can serve many purposes. In addition to bringing publicity to an area of the institution, an online exhibition that highlights, say, recent acquisitions or a new building will help to raise staff morale. The ability to take something like a recent acquisition or a quick library history and turn it into an online exhibition or display can often be done simply and by staff who may not regularly work on full-fledged gallery exhibitions. A fine example of a library history exhibition comes from Houston Public Library. This exhibition, the *History of the Houston Public Library,* is a simple narrative history of the library interspersed with photographs of the library's various buildings, events, and staff.

A much different approach to this type of exhibition idea is seen in *Keeping Our Word: Preserving Information across the Ages* from the University of Iowa Libraries. This exhibition, which "celebrates the myriad efforts made over time to preserve information," both serves as an exhibition of the work being done in preservation at the University of Iowa Libraries and provides a fascinating overview of the preservation of library and archival materials.

In addition to being able to celebrate their own work and staff, libraries and archives are often in a unique position to highlight the history of their parent institutions or their staff. The Perry Library at Old Dominion University and the Harvey Library at Hampton University worked together to create *From Exposition to Development: The Legacy of Composers at Hampton University,* which uses images and archival documents to trace the contributions of five composers to the music composition heritage of Virginia.

Odd and Unusual

Though all of the above make wonderful topics for online exhibitions, sometimes it is the odd and the unusual that will both educate and entertain your online exhibition visitors. A good example of this is *Celebrating the Boar* from the University of Waterloo Library. Taking as its starting point a seven-hundred-pound bronze boar statue donated by a faculty member, the exhibition goes on to examine the role of the boar in art and in history.

Only from Las Vegas could come the exhibition *Dino at the Sands,* an exploration of the life and career of Dean Martin from the UNLV Libraries Special Collections (see figure 7). A similar exhibition, *The Jackie Gleason Collection,* from the University of Miami's Otto G. Richter Library, focuses not on the entertainer's show business career but rather on his collection of occult and parapsychology materials, which he donated to the library.

FIGURE 7 | *Dino at the Sands.* UNLV Libraries Special Collections.

ALL EXHIBITION IDEAS' TIME IS NOT RIPE

Michael Belcher (1991, 37), in *Exhibitions in Museums,* defines an exhibition as "'showing for a purpose,' the purpose being to affect the viewer in some predetermined way." Though we have outlined a host of potential ideas, it needs to be said that not all ideas are created equal and that some ideas are best left in the closet of their thinker's mind, never to see the light of day, virtual or otherwise.

An idea might not be suitable for an exhibition for a number of reasons. The library or archive may not have, or may not be able to borrow, the proper objects to see the idea through to completion. In other cases, the objects themselves may not be suitable for use in an exhibition. The fragility of an object is of less concern in an online exhibition than in a gallery exhibition. Still, the physical state of an object may keep it from being either directly digitized or photographed for secondary digitization.

Lastly, even the best of ideas cannot be converted into an online exhibition if the proper support and staff are not behind it.

DEVELOPMENT OF THE EXHIBITION IDEA

Rare is the idea that, like Athena, springs forth fully formed from the head of Zeus. Once the initial idea for an exhibition is settled on, the idea will need to be further developed. Development includes vigorously analyzing the idea and teasing out all its possibilities. Examine the idea from all sides and angles to see what additional elements can be added from the collections to flesh it out in an online environment.

Librarians and archivists, particularly special collections librarians and curators, can never hope to "fling wide the golden gates and let the public in" (Low 1942, 7) to the totality of their collections. With the right idea and the proper execution, however, your collections can take on a new life and generate a whole new audience.

SOURCES CITED

Canadian Heritage Information Network. *Internet Virtual Exhibition Production Reference Guide.* Available at: http://www.chin.gc.ca/ Exhibitions/Virtual_Guide/indexa.html.

Low, Theodore. 1942. *The Museum as a Social Instrument.* New York: Metropolitan Museum of Art. Quoted in Michael Belcher, *Exhibitions in Museums* (Washington, D.C.: Smithsonian Institution Press, 1991).

ONLINE EXHIBITIONS DISCUSSED

American Treasures of the Library of Congress. Library of Congress.
  http://lcweb.loc.gov/exhibits/treasures

California Pacific Exposition: San Diego 1935–1936. San Diego Historical
  Society.
  http://www.sandiegohistory.org/calpac/index.htm

Canada at Scale: Maps of Our History. National Archives of Canada / Archives
  nationales du Canada.
  http://www.archives.ca/05/0514_e.html

*The Capture of Fort William and Mary, New Castle, New Hampshire, December
  14–15, 1774.* University of New Hampshire Library, Milne Special
  Collections and Archives.
  http://www.izaak.unh.edu/specoll/exhibits/1774.htm

The Cartographic Creation of New England. University of Southern Maine,
  Osher Map Library and Smith Center for Cartographic Education.
  http://www.usm.maine.edu/~maps/exhibit2

Celebrating the Boar. University of Waterloo Library.
  http://www.lib.uwaterloo.ca/tour/boar/BoarContents.html

The Chicago Fire. Chicago Historical Society.
  http://www.chicagohistory.org/history/fire.html

Children's Books of the Early Soviet Era: Yesterday, Today and . . . Tomorrow.
  Rare Books and Special Collections Division, McGill University Libraries.
  http://imago.library.mcgill.ca/russian

Churchill: The Evidence. National Library of Scotland and the Churchill
  Archives Centre.
  http://www.churchill.nls.ac.uk

The Common Wealth: Treasures from the Collections of the Library of Virginia.
  Library of Virginia.
  http://www.lva.lib.va.us/sb/exhibits/treasures/index.htm

Connies. State Library of Victoria (Australia).
  http://www.slv.vic.gov.au/slv/exhibitions/connies

Dino at the Sands. UNLV Libraries Special Collections.
  http://library.nevada.edu/speccol/dino/index.html

The Dr. Charles Wolf Collection of Irish Postage Stamps. Department of Rare
  Books and Special Collections, University of Notre Dame Library.
  http://www.rarebooks.nd.edu/stamps/irish

Dr. Seuss Went to War: A Catalog of Political Cartoons by Dr. Seuss. University
  of California, San Diego, Mandeville Special Collections Library.
  http://orpheus.ucsd.edu/speccoll/dspolitic/index.htm

The Earth and the Heavens: The Art of the Mapmaker. British Library.
> http://portico.bl.uk/exhibitions/maps

The Enduring Legacy of Paper Bindings. New York University, Fales Library and Special Collections.
> http://www.nyu.edu/library/bobst/research/preserv/lecture/paper.htm

Exploring Africa: An Exhibit of Maps and Travel Narratives. University of South Carolina, Thomas Cooper Library.
> http://www.sc.edu/library/spcoll/sccoll/africa/africa.html

1492: An Ongoing Voyage. Library of Congress.
> http://lcweb.loc.gov/exhibits/1492/intro.html

From Exposition to Development: The Legacy of Composers at Hampton University. Perry Library at Old Dominion University and Harvey Library at Hampton University.
> http://www.lib.odu.edu/aboutlib/musiclib/exhibits/hamptonex/
> onlinex.html

From Smithson to Smithsonian. Smithsonian Institution Libraries.
> http://www.sil.si.edu/Exhibitions/Smithson-to-Smithsonian

Fruits of a Research Collection. Texas A&M University, Cushing Library.
> http://library.tamu.edu/cushing/onlinex/fruits/intro.html

Girls Fight for a Living. University of Louisville, Ekstrom Library Photograph Archives.
> http://athena.louisville.edu/library/ekstrom/special/girls/girls.html

Highlights of the Map Collection, National Library of Scotland. National Library of Scotland.
> http://www.nls.ac.uk/digitallibrary/map/map.htm

The History of Railway Photography. National Railway Museum (Great Britain).
> http://www.nrm.org.uk/html/exhib_pb/photo/start.htm

History of the Houston Public Library. Houston Public Library.
> http://sparc.hpl.lib.tx.us/hpl/libhist.html

Irish Treasures from the O'Hegarty Irish Collection. University of Kansas Libraries, Department of Special Collections of the Kenneth Spencer Research Library.
> http://www.spencer.lib.ku.edu/exhibits/irish_treasures/shamrock.html

The Jackie Gleason Collection. University of Miami, Otto G. Richter Library.
> http://www.library.miami.edu/archives/jg/index.html

Keeping Our Word: Preserving Information across the Ages. University of Iowa Libraries.

http://www.lib.uiowa.edu/ref/exhibit/index.html

The Night before Christmas by Clement C. Moore, Illustrated. Brown University Library.

http://www.brown.edu/Facilities/University_Library/exhibits/
TNBC/tnbc.html

1997: A Year of Many Anniversaries. Oregon State University, Archives and Records Management Program.

http://osu.orst.edu/Dept/archives/exhibits/yrspast/yrspast.htm

Treasures from Europe's National Libraries. Conference of European National Librarians.

http://www.ddb.de/gabriel/treasures/entree.html

Treasures of Florida Libraries: A Celebration of Rare and Unique Materials. University of Miami Library.

http://www.library.miami.edu/treasure/treasure.html

Treasures of the APS. American Philosophical Society.

http://www.amphilsoc.org/library/exhibits/treasures

Treasures of the Royal Library. Klenodier fra Det kgl. Bibliotek (Denmark).

http://www.kb.dk/kultur/expo/klenod

219 Loyola: Building a Library for New Orleans. New Orleans Public Library.

http://nutrias.org/~nopl/exhibits/219/219.htm

CHAPTER 3

Executing the Exhibition Idea

The people's museum should be much more than a house full of specimens in glass cases. It should be a house full of ideas, arranged with the strictest attention to system.—George Brown Goode

Once you have a general idea of a concept that will form an online exhibition, you will need to analyze the exhibition idea. Focus on the key elements of the idea, the objects, and the script that will transform the idea into an exhibition. In some cases, what you once thought to be a great idea will fall short when you find that you do not have the objects to support the idea. At other times, the idea and the objects are in place, but an adequate exhibition script cannot be created to properly tie everything together. In the worst cases, objects and script will fail the idea (whatever were you thinking in the first place?), and in the best of cases, objects and script will fall together almost as if by magic and the online exhibition will appear to the world in a wondrous digital epiphany. (Note: this will not happen very often!)

The exhibition planning process is composed of a number of distinct steps. In the case of libraries and archives with an ongoing gallery exhibition program, many of the planning steps may already be outlined in internal policies and procedures. With a little bit of adaptation, these policies and procedures may be adapted to reflect the special needs of online exhibitions.

Some of the general steps that should be followed in an online exhibition planning process include:

Preparation of the exhibition proposal

Proposal evaluation

Selection of objects

Drafting of the script

Preparation of objects

Exhibition design and Web creation

Final editing

Additions, changes, corrections

EXHIBITION POLICIES

A key component of any exhibition program, either gallery based or virtual, is a clear and well-defined exhibition policy. A good exhibition policy will lay out the mission and goals of a library or archives exhibition program and allow staff to have a clear idea of what is expected in an exhibition and how it fits into the larger mission of the institution.

An exhibition policy should explain how exhibitions contribute to outreach and the presentation of library and archival materials often not available to a larger audience. The exhibition policy can also explain how the selection of books, manuscripts, graphics, and objects will address topics of historical and cultural interest. How proposals are evaluated (whether by the director, an exhibition officer, or a team assigned exhibition responsibilities) is important. A collegiality in proposal review, with the opportunity for potential curators to receive feedback on their proposals, will increase the quality of all ensuing exhibitions. Though some proposals will be accepted quickly without further review or revision, at other times, the kernel of a good idea will be present in a proposal but will need further development before it can grow into a viable online exhibition. Any proposal evaluation should have in place a methodology for nurturing promising, but presently lacking, proposals. And lastly, the policy should outline staff responsibilities, standards, and general formats that should be employed in the exhibitions.

Exhibition Policy Outline

A library and archival exhibition policy could address the elements below. (Though many of these elements will be relevant to both gallery and online exhibitions, the online elements will be the major focus.)

Purpose.   What are the reasons for creating exhibitions in your institution? Examples might include promoting interest in the collections, presenting rare or fragile materials, or educating users in the use of the collections.

Content.   What type of content will be used in the exhibitions? Generally, the majority of the objects in an exhibition will be from the library or archive itself. To address cases in which objects may be borrowed from other institutions or from individuals, the policy may comment on the balance of borrowed versus owned objects that will be displayed.

Standards.   What are the standards (in terms of intellectual content, presentation, and so forth) that will be used for your institution's exhibitions? A few standards that you may keep in mind that may automatically apply to your exhibitions include those related to *accessibility* (how the exhibition program will comply with the Americans with Disabilities Act regulations) and other *policies* or *directives* your library or archive (or their parent institution) maintains in regard to exhibitions.

Authority and Responsibility.   An exhibition policy *must* clearly outline the areas of responsibility for exhibitions. In most cases, the *director* will have final authority and responsibility for the library's or archive's exhibitions (that's why they get paid more than the rest of us!). The director, however, will delegate the work to appropriate staff, reserving final approval for him- or herself. An *administrative librarian* or officer will need to have duties such as budgeting, staffing, and other coordinating functions. In institutions with large and ongoing exhibition programs (most gallery exhibition programs), an *exhibitions officer* will manage the day-to-day running of the exhibition program. Responsibilities in this area would include *content management* (approving and selecting curators and working with the curators on exhibition content) and *scheduling and implementation* (coordinating materials, space, and the like). In many cases, the exhibitions officer will come from the special collections or similar department. The *curator* is the heart of the exhibition and the one responsible for the exhibition's intellectual content, scholarly accuracy, and general organization. The policy should also assign an *editorial* position to ensure that scripts and text meet the standards of the institution. The editorial position may also coordinate with the curator any publicity for the exhibition.

THE EXHIBITION PROPOSAL

With the guidance of an exhibition policy in place, the first step for exhibition planners will be the writing of an exhibition proposal. Even in those cases where a formal proposal does not need to be submitted to the institution's administration, writing a proposal can help to clarify the exhibition in the curator's mind, guide the ongoing creation of the exhibition, and, in some necessary cases, stop work on the idea. Additionally, a good proposal will help with any fund-raising if supplemental funds are needed for the exhibition.

Among the elements of a good exhibition proposal are

Title and theme	Staff
Purpose	Budget
Audience	Timeline(s)
Design	Preliminary object list
Maintenance	

Title and Theme.   Though an exhibition is not a dissertation or even a book on a subject, its title should strive to convey what it is all about. There should also be a short summary of the themes presented in the exhibition.

Purpose.   What is the purpose of this exhibition? Is it merely pretty pictures? Or does it strive to tell a story? In this portion of the proposal you should discuss the idea behind the exhibition (an anniversary, a notable event, specific materials, a theme, treasures) and the approach that will be taken (aesthetic, emotive, evocative, didactic, entertaining).

Audience.   There are many potential audiences for an online exhibition, and it will be impossible for any single exhibition to target them all. The more clearly your audience is defined, the more focused the exhibition will become. When thinking about audience, keep in mind such issues as local versus global appeal, knowledge levels about the subject, reading levels, and language. Recognition and understanding of the audience for your exhibition (whether a current audience that you hope to retain or a new audience that you are cultivating) is important. On the one hand, do not focus on so narrow an audience that your exhibition appeals to only a few visitors. On the other hand, "the whole world" is not a good choice either. Though a single exhibition will never be able to meet the needs and expectations of all potential audiences, remember that with the Web, much of your work can easily be repurposed. In many cases, the same images can be used for exhibition scripts that target different audiences. Lastly, one should consider both the technical skills and the hardware/software/bandwidth capabilities of your potential audience.

Design.   Though each exhibition will (and should) have its own unique look and feel, in many instances there will be a house style that will be adhered to for at least certain elements (for example, the use and placement of institutional logos or color schemes). A good exhibition proposal, however, will include some notion of what the curator has in mind for the presentation of his or her idea. This will be of assistance to the designer at a later point in the exhibition process.

Maintenance.   The Web does not set a single version of an exhibition in stone. An exhibition has an opening date (when it will become available to the public), but it need never close. The temptation of the relative ease with which an online exhibition may be edited or corrected can lead to an expectation that elements can be changed or added to later. Some types of exhibitions will be greatly enhanced by periodic updating and refreshing. If the curator feels that the exhibition has the potential of benefiting from updating, this should be noted in the proposal. Curators, should, however, beware the example of Henry James, whose rewriting and editing of his early novels (when they were republished in the New York edition near the end of his life) are frowned upon by both scholars and the common reader.

Staff.   The curator should note what staff in addition to him- or herself may need to work on the project. In institutions with formerly established exhibition teams or committees this will be an easier process. Remember that teams can offer staff a chance to exercise talents and exhibit creativity not shown in day-to-day work. Potential makeup of such teams is noted in chapter 4.

Budget.   The curator should make an estimate of any unusual needs or services that the exhibition may necessitate. Standard and usual costs associated with digitizing (which will be outlined later) probably will not need to be noted at this point. If, however, the curator is expecting to utilize new or different technologies that have not been used in past exhibitions (audio and video being two examples), a note on potential monetary and staff-time investments should be made.

Timeline(s).   In libraries and archives, the majority of curators are going to have regular, full-time jobs (cataloger, reference librarian, collection processor). Creating an online exhibition can be a time-consuming and intellectually laborious task. A good proposal will take into account work and life and present a firm timeline for delivering scripts, script revisions, and supplemental materials (bibliographies and the like) to the design staff.

Preliminary Object List.   A list of objects (books, manuscripts, photographs, and so forth) that the curator plans to put in the exhibition will help the reader picture how the objects will flesh out the narrative of the script. In most cases, the object list does not have to be complete or thorough. As the script develops, objects may be added or dropped from the exhibition. In some instances, an object may need to be replaced when it is found to be unsuitable for digitizing; in others, the story of an object may not contribute to the totality of the exhibition's narrative.

A thorough and well-planned exhibition proposal will make the task of creating the online exhibition easier for all involved. Spending extra time during the proposal stage will save time later, when the final presentation of the exhibition is actually executed. For an example of an online exhibition proposal, see appendix A.

DEFINING THE IDEA

Organizing an Exhibition Site

Once your exhibition proposal has been accepted and the wheels of the exhibition have been set in motion, it's time to start to work on the script and the final selection of objects. As you begin to work more closely with the ideas and the objects, you will need to determine an organizational structure for your exhibition.

Gallery exhibitions are spaces where visitors may move freely (even exhibitions with strong linear arrangements that take a visitor on a path through the display). Instead of following the strict, conventional narrative of a novel (or television program or movie), gallery exhibitions, with their ability to allow the viewer to pick and choose what to read, what objects to look at, and what order to look at objects in, present, in a sense, a form of hypernarrative more akin to web browsing.

In a gallery exhibition, visitors are tempted by other exhibitions, restaurants, gift shops, and rest rooms. Similarly, in an online exhibition, the visitors' ability to move around the site (and even off the site!) makes some sort of organization necessary to keep them from getting lost.

As with gallery exhibitions, there are numerous possibilities for organizing your idea and objects. Among these possibilities are

Object-oriented organization

Systematic organization

Thematic organization

Organization by material type

Organization by multiple schemes

Object-Oriented Organization. In an object-oriented exhibition, there is a simple presentation of the objects with little systematic organization. In an exhibition of this type, the objects and their descriptions remain the chief focus. Though there may be some sort of simple organization (such as alphabetical or chronological), the organization remains secondary to the presentation of the objects. Exhibitions devoted to treasures or recent acquisitions make good candidates for this method of organization. An example of an object-oriented exhibition is *Recent Acquisitions in NCSU Libraries' Special Collections, 1998–1999,* from North Carolina State University. In this exhibition, 16 of the 550 new acquisitions from the NSCU Special Collections are highlighted in a simple presentation with a few images and a short descriptive text.

Systematic Organization. A systematically organized exhibition can be arranged in a variety of ways. A common form of systematic organization is *chronological order.* Chronological exhibitions tell their story by starting at the beginning (a very good place to start!) and moving through time to the end. Among the many examples of a chronological exhibition are *Reflections in Time,* from Middle Tennessee State University. This exhibition traces the history and growth of the university from 1911 through 1999 in photographs, objects, and other material. Another form of a systematic organization is *taxonomic,* where related objects are grouped together (either directly or through hierarchies). *Daughter of Earth: Agnes Smedley and Smedley-MacKinnon Collections,* from the Department of Archives and Manuscripts, Arizona State University Libraries, gives a brief view of the life of the famous radical. Topics such as "College Life" and "In China" are used to outline Smedley's story. Groups of photographs are arranged on each topic.

Executing the Exhibition Idea

Thematic Organization. A thematically organized exhibition is structured around themes and/or tells a story. *Oveta Culp Hobby, the Little Colonel,* from the Woodson Research Center, Special Collections at Fondren Library, Rice University, explores the life of Hobby, the first director of the Women's Army Auxiliary Corps (WAAC). Through a narrative structure interspersed with photographs and documents, the viewer can explore the early history of the WAACs as well as Hobby's life. Another thematic exhibition is *Science and the Artist's Book,* from Smithsonian Institution Libraries (see figure 8). This exhibition is built around the theme of artists' books inspired by volumes from the Heralds of Science collection of the Dibner Library of the History of Science and Technology.

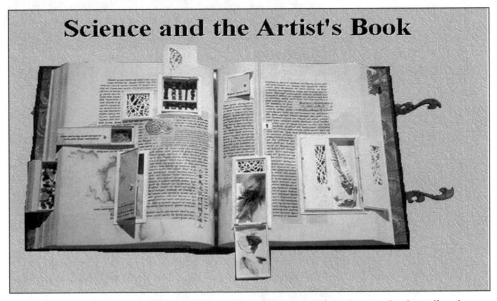

FIGURE 8 | *Science and the Artist's Book.* Courtesy Smithsonian Institution Libraries.

Organization by Material Type. In some exhibitions, organizing all the objects by their original material type will provide the viewer with the best presentation. *Nos Los Inquisidores,* from the Department of Special Collections of the University Libraries of Notre Dame, is built around a selection from the 564 objects in the Harley L. McDevitt Inquisition Collection (see figure 9). Arrangement by such topics as "Indices of Banned Books," "Autos-da-fé," and "Official Publications" allows the viewer to explore the exhibition not in a strict linear manner but by picking and choosing from the types of materials available.

Organization by Multiple Schemes. One of the beauties of the Web, of course, is that multiple methods of organization can be applied to an exhibition.

FIGURE 9 | *Nos Los Inquisidores.* Reproduced with permission from the website of the Department of Special Collections of the University Libraries of Notre Dame.

In *Frontier Photographer: Edward S. Curtis* (figure 10), from Smithsonian Institution Libraries, for example, the viewer can follow a roughly chronological progression of Curtis's life or jump around through such categories as "Early Life," "Family Sacrifices," "Early Books," and "Alaska."

It is important to remember that you must try and maintain a coherent organization to your exhibition. An exhibition without a major organizing principle can often degenerate into a mere random collection of images or provide the viewer with so many choices for navigating the site that there is no clear vision of the exhibition's theme.

FIGURE 10 | *Frontier Photographer: Edward S. Curtis.* Courtesy Smithsonian Institution Libraries.

SELECTION OF OBJECTS

Museum exhibitions remind one of a quick-lunch bar, where the guests see not only what they consume, but can also discern the ingredients of which the food is being prepared.—Emil Horn

What menu choices do you want to offer at the lunch counter of your online exhibition? Or, more precisely, what types of objects should one put in an exhibition? Obviously, the choices will be made from your collections (or from objects borrowed from other collections) that illustrate the theme of your exhibition. The ancillary criteria that go into selecting objects for an exhibition,

Executing the Exhibition Idea

and especially for an online exhibition, however, are quite varied and should be explored in greater detail. The visitor will be attracted to dramatic objects when presented with a host of them to look at in greater detail (Belcher 1991, 111). Or, as similarly stated by John Cotton Dana, librarian and museum pioneer, "objects are silent" (1927, 16).

A stunning and dramatic object can, even in an online exhibition, leave vivid impressions on the viewer. Library and archival objects are in many ways well suited to online presentation. Unlike the majority of three-dimensional artifacts found in the typical museum exhibition, books, manuscripts, photographs, and other basically flat materials do not lose as much of their *presence* when rendered as images on a screen. This is not to say, however, that viewing a page of the *Book of Kells* or the Declaration of Independence in 75 dpi on a 15-inch monitor will ever provide the same thrill as viewing those items in person.

Now, for a quick vocabulary lesson. What is the difference between an *exhibit* and an *exhibition*? In the common parlance (and even frequently in museum publications), the two words are interchangeable. For purposes of clarity, however, the following distinctions between the two should be made: an *exhibit* is "one element or component of a larger group or a single, standalone experience"; an *exhibition* is a "group of elements, planned as a cohesive unit, under a specified theme or topic" (Serrell 1998, 12). In this section, the terms *exhibit* and *object* are used interchangeably.

Object Selection

Belcher (1991, 147) notes that the "most likely reasons for selecting an object for exhibition are that, in the opinion of the curator, the object is intrinsically of interest, or information about it is considered of value to the visitor, or the object has a contribution to make to a more general story which the visitor is to be told."

In most instances, the idea for the exhibition, the definition of the idea, and the selection of the objects are all closely related to one another as well as to the writing of the script. What, however, lies behind the selection of certain objects for certain exhibitions? A few quotations from selected exhibitions may offer some enlightenment.

For an exhibition of Whitman materials, the curators selected "artifacts of a fascinating and extremely dynamic period of American publishing history" (*Walt Whitman and the Development of "Leaves of Grass,"* University of South Carolina Libraries, Department of Rare Books and Special Collections). From *The Writings of Paul Laurence Dunbar* exhibition at a public library comes this statement on object selection: "Springfield Library's Rare Book and Special Collections room is fortunate to own seventeen first editions of Dunbar's books, published during his lifetime. This represents the vast majority of the books issued before his death. The purpose of this exhibit is to display these wonderful books together and simultaneously inspire a renewal of interest in this important American poet and novelist."

As a last example, the Yale University Library's exhibition *A Great Assemblage: An Exhibit of Judaica* (figure 11) notes that the objects were selected in the hope that the exhibition will "present in miniature the depth and richness of Yale's vast Hebraica and Judaica holdings."

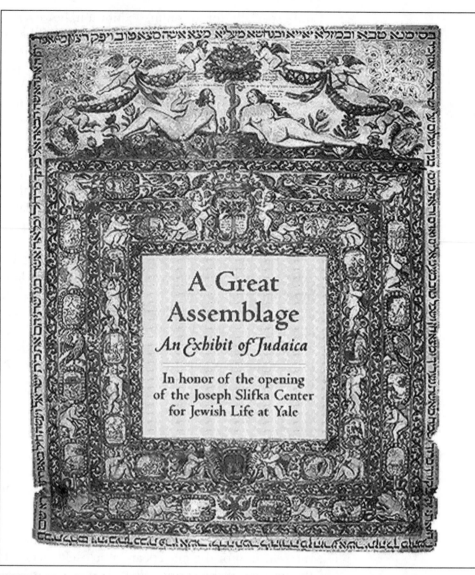

FIGURE 11 | Jewish marriage contract, Nice, 1690, from the Yale University Library Judaica Collection exhibit "A Great Assemblage," 1995. http://www.library.yale.edu/exhibition/Judaica.

Preparation of Objects

Once the first selection of objects for an exhibition has been made, preparation of those objects for digitization can begin. Details about the actual digitization of objects will be discussed later, but two things to keep in mind as objects are selected are as follows:

Will the object need any special conservation treatment before it can be used for the exhibition?

Is the object needed for any other purpose for which its absence during the digitization process will cause a hardship?

In the case of a gallery exhibition that will simultaneously become an online exhibition, it is extremely important that the objects be either digitized or photographed well before they will be needed for the installation of the gallery exhibition.

WRITING THE EXHIBITION SCRIPT

Now, with your idea in place, your proposal approved, and your preliminary list of objects prepared, it's time to start the real work, the writing of the script.

As you begin to write the script, if you keep your organization in mind, the process will move along more easily because you can use the organization as a sort of outline. The preparation of the script itself will fall roughly into four areas:

Original draft
Approval process
Additions/changes/corrections
Final draft

Elements of the Script

Like any form of writing, an exhibition script has a number of predefined elements that nearly all scripts will include. Depending upon the nature of your exhibition, you may choose to exclude certain of these elements; however, in nearly all instances, you will include most of the following:

Narrative
Pull quotes
Object labels
Object captions
Statement of authorship or responsibility
Credits and acknowledgments

When you first approach a gallery exhibition, you will often find on the wall outside the gallery text that provides a general introduction to the exhibition. As you move through the gallery space, you will find additional text that moves you through the exhibition or that provides transition between different segments of the exhibition. This portion of the script is the *narrative*. For the viewer, narrative text both outlines and ties together the objects in the exhibition. In the New York Public Library's exhibition *The Romanovs: Their Empire, Their Books. The Political, Religious, Cultural, and Social Life of Russia's Imperial House*, a brief narrative text provides the transition between the major sections of the exhibition:

> Up to the fall of the Romanovs in 1917, the Russians were the largest population group in the empire. Their representation and ways were therefore of prime interest to members of the dynasty. Among the more than one hundred other peoples or ethnic groups in the empire, only a few seemed significant enough—by virtue of their location, numbers, or quaintness—to deserve attention, so imperial libraries contain only a limited and very selective literature dealing with them. Travel books enabled their owners to extend their knowledge and to document their own visits to some regions of the realm.

The narrative portion of your script is where you will begin to assemble the research and data collected during exhibition planning and where you will further develop the statement that reflects the theme chosen for the exhibition.

Pull quotes, text taken from the narrative of the script or from objects, often serve as transitions between portions of narrative text. They can also highlight the themes, ideas, and structure of the exhibition. When doing research for the exhibition, the curator should be on the lookout for appropriate quotes or catchy text that can be used as exhibition pull quotes. Numerous examples of pull quotes may be found in *Frontier Photographer: Edward S. Curtis* from Smithsonian Institution Libraries.

Object labels and object captions are closely related but serve different purposes. An *object caption* is often a brief bit of text, as in this example from the Maine Historical Society's *Rum, Riot, and Reform: Maine and the History of American Drinking:*

> **Bangor House**
> Joseph F. Hatch, 1883
> Oil on canvas
> Collections of the Bangor Historical Society

From the same exhibition comes the accompanying *object label:*

> Maine's grand city hotel is said to have always served
> liquor by simply paying fines as the cost of doing business.
> In Portland, J. B. Brown's Falmouth Hotel reportedly
> practiced the same method.

The object caption is just that, a brief summary that explains what the object is, where it comes from, and in some cases, its media and format. In an online exhibition, object captions will generally appear as text located near the image of the object. Additionally, in many cases, the caption text will be embedded in the digital image. A chief benefit of embedding caption information in the digital image is that often visitors may stumble upon the images via search engines or in some other manner. When caption information is embedded in the image, if the object is ever orphaned, the viewer will have some idea of what it is and where it came from. See, for example, figure 12, which shows an embedded caption from the Smithsonian Institution Libraries' exhibition *"Make the Dirt Fly!"*

Basic information that you *must* present for each object in your online exhibition (either in the object caption itself or in a linked file) includes

What it is

Where it is

Credit and copyright information

What It Is. For books, this information should include, at minimum, author, title, and year of publication. If more space is available, you may also want to include publisher, place of publication, original size, and similar useful facts. For other types of objects (manuscripts, photographs, and so forth), be as inclusive yet as concise as possible. Remember that with an online exhibition, you can easily accommodate a checklist of objects displayed. That is where you can let your catalogers run wild and include thorough and comprehensive bibliographic citations.

Panama Pacific International Exposition San Francisco, 1915, by Panama Pacific International Exposition Co., 1914
Smithsonian Institution Libraries

FIGURE 12 | World's Fair literature from *"Make the Dirt Fly!"* Courtesy Smithsonian Institution Libraries.

Where It Is. Is the item from your own collections? Don't assume the viewer will just know. Also, don't assume that all your visitors will know that the original photographs are held in special collections, the photo archive, or other specialty locations. Give as much information as possible on where in your collections a given object resides so that viewers can visit your library to see the object in person. Or, if you ever need to retrieve the specific item, a call number or other specific locator for the item should be included.

Credit and Copyright Information. Given the slough of copyright rules and regulations, it is best to include a statement of some sort cleared through your institution's legal counsel. For objects borrowed from other institutions (and for which you received permission for inclusion in an online exhibition), your lending agreement may require a very specific credit line. Examples of credit lines include

Collections of Suzanne Messier, Michel-Pierre Sarrazin, Loto-Québec, René Derouin, and Glenbow Museum (from the exhibition *Frontiers, Frontières, Fronteras: René Derouin*)

Courtesy of Ianus Publications (from the exhibition *Out of This World: Canadian Science Fiction and Fantasy*)

Early Printed Collections, The British Library (from the exhibition *John Bull and Uncle Sam: Four Centuries of British-American Relations*)

For nonbook or archival objects, include as much information as possible to help in identification (as in the caption for the bill hopper in figure 13). Answer the following questions about the object (as appropriate): What is it? When was it made? What is it made of? How was it made? Where was it made? What is its function? What is its significance? What is its physical description (size, weight, other dimensions)? (Belcher 1991, 151, 153).

The object label differs from the object caption in that it provides more extensive and contextualized information about an object. When writing your object labels, remember, as quoted previously from John Cotton Dana, that objects are silent. In an online exhibition, the object label takes on additional importance, as viewers will not have key visual cues to assist them with understanding an object. For example, in the Smithsonian Institution Libraries'

Senate Bill Hopper
Mahogany, 1838–1846
190.5h × 59.4w × 59.7d cm (75h × 23 3/8w × 23 1/2d in)

Bill hopper, 1838-46. National Museum of American History, Smithsonian Institution

Digital image (c) 1996 Smithsonian Institution

FIGURE 13 | Bill hopper from *From Smithson to Smithsonian.* Courtesy Smithsonian Institution Libraries.

exhibition *From Smithson to Smithsonian,* what at first glance appears to be a chair of indeterminate size becomes, once one has read the object label and caption, a Senate bill hopper (see figure 13).

> **Object Caption**
> Senate Bill Hopper
> Mahogany, 1838–1846
> 190.5h × 59.4w × 59.7d cm (75h × 23 3/8w × 23 1/2d in)
>
> **Object Label**
> This U.S. Senate bill hopper offers clear evidence of how few bills actually became law. The upper shelves—which represent the final phases of legislative consideration—were built to accommodate the fewest bills.

Everyone likes to get credit for the work they've done. In an online exhibition, however, it is necessity and not vanity that dictates the including of a *statement of authorship or responsibility.* An online exhibition, like any exhibition or other work of scholarly or entertainment value, draws its validity from who created it. To take an extreme example, *The Many Talents of John Gorham Palfrey, Our First Dean,* from Andover-Harvard Theological Library, has much more respectability because of its association with the library and a named curator (Clifford Wunderlich) than it would have if it had been done by, say, a Yale Bulldog frat house. Remember the old Internet joke: "On the Internet, no one knows you're a dog." By the same token, to establish identity and validity, you must take pains to announce that you are not just any old dog, but a Westminster Kennel Club Champion!

Credits and acknowledgments can be separated into two sections or kept as a single, integrated whole. Credits will be used specifically to thank those that assisted with the preparation of the exhibition. It is here where the different members of the exhibition team can be credited for their work. The acknowledgments section is where other staff members who may have made a contribution to the exhibition (such as the student assistants who helped with the research and the staff who went out of their way to help you find just the right book for the exhibition) can be thanked. It is also where institutions that receive additional financial support for the online exhibition (or for the original gallery exhibition upon which the online version may have been based) may thank donors. Note: the entire issue of providing benefactors' names in an online environment can be a tricky one. You may wish to check with your legal counsel or development office on policies and procedures for crediting supporters online.

Revision of the Script

Once you have completed the entire script (narrative, labels, captions, and all), it is time to begin the reviewing process. In some institutions or for certain types of exhibitions that may be culturally or politically sensitive, you may wish to have the script reviewed by an outside expert. Complex exhibitions that propound new or revised scholarly theory may benefit from a peer review process, as used for articles in professional journals. Any appropriate suggestions, comments, changes, or corrections should then be incorporated into the script.

After the intellectual content and organization of the script is settled on, make certain that your script gets a thorough review for spelling and grammar. You may also wish to run the script through a second level of fact checking at this point. (How many times do you have to remind yourself whether it was synthetic or analytic cubism that came first!)

When doing the final review, keep in mind the flow of the script. The flow will include the interrelationship of all the parts of the exhibition as well as the overall clarity of the presentation and the relationship of the parts to the theme.

See appendix B for a sample exhibition script.

A Further Discussion of Exhibit Labels

Before we proceed to our next topic, a further discussion of the art of writing exhibit labels is in order. As George Brown Goode noted in 1891 (432), "each object must bear a label, giving its name and history so fully that all the probable questions of the visitor are answered in advance." Literally dozens of books and many dozens of articles have been written on how to create exhibit labels.

Those who write museum labels for a living will tell you that it is its own unique art form and perhaps should exist as its own genre, like fiction, poetry, and advertising. The form and function of the mode of communication makes all the difference. In the case of a book, the author uses many thousands of words to get across his purpose (whether it is to inform or to entertain); in a poem, the poet typically uses far fewer words but often has ideas that are just as complex or even more complex to communicate. In an advertisement, the number of words may be negligible, but each word must sell the product. In an exhibit label, the number of words is similar to that of a poem or an advertisement, and those words must, on some levels, both communicate a complex idea and sell a product (in this case, keep the attention of the viewer). At the same time, the label must be "interesting, readable, legible, and deserving of visitors' attention" (Serrell 1982, v). Also remember that, as David Bearman (1995) has noted, "people do not want the things in themselves, they want the meaning they convey."

Beverly Serrell, who has written extensively on exhibit labels, enumerates eight deadly sins of exhibit labels. Though some of those sins pertain only to gallery exhibitions, many of the flaws of a bad gallery label can be replicated online. Serrell (1982, 19) specifically criticizes labels that are

Too long and wordy

Too technical for the intended readers

Boring, with inappropriate information

Badly edited, with mistakes in grammar, spelling, or syntax

Too small—tiny words crammed on a three-inch-by-five-inch card

Hard to read (the result of poor typography)

Colored in a way that makes reading difficult or tiresome

Badly placed, causing neck, back, or eye strain in the viewer

Likewise, Stephen C. Bitgood (1986, 3–9) has commented on the factors that are important in creating a successful exhibit label. Bitgood delineates four groups that need to be considered in the writing of exhibit labels. They are visitors, staff, content experts, and stylistic experts. Each of these groups will have a different stake in the content and formulation of a label. When considering the visitor, the writer thinks about the number of visitors or viewers that will actually read a particular label, the amount of time a visitor will spend reading the label (its holding power), the knowledge a visitor will gain from the label, and whether the information on the label will stimulate the visitor to delve deeper into the subject (or at least continue with the exhibition).

For the other groups, there will be different consideration. For staff (and in the case of an online exhibition, this would include the creators of the exhibition as well as other library or archives staff who may view the exhibition), the content and attractiveness of the label are important. For content experts (who may reside within your institution or be visitors who find your exhibition somewhere on the Web), the key element of an exhibit label is the accuracy of its facts. For the stylistic expert, a label will fail if it does not conform to acceptable standards of grammatical usage (to the more easygoing and hyperinformal writers out there, members of this group will be known as the pickers of nit).

In an online exhibition, labels for the objects will allow the curator to expand the amount of information available. Callery and Thibadeau (2000), in "On Beyond Label Copy," note that "access to the content of the archival documents . . . can be provided based on the user's expressed level of interest similar to the selection made for a traditional on-the-walls exhibition or in a less-structured way similar to that of users browsing a library catalog."

All the elements, good and bad, noted above and in the literature of exhibit labeling generally pertain to gallery exhibitions. Let's now take a closer look at some of the concerns and special requirements of the script and labels for an online exhibition.

The Online Environment

How does an online exhibition differ from a gallery exhibition? Some of the differences are obvious. Visitors have less control over their environment in an online exhibition. Objects for the most part will appear only as two-dimensional images on a screen (leaving aside for the moment the possibility of three-dimensional imaging, which, though it simulates three dimensions, is still presenting objects on a flat screen).

Physical "exhibitions are conceived as sculpture. They are three-dimensional compositions which recognize the importance of solids and voids and strive for satisfactory spatial relationships" (Belcher 1991, 41). Online exhibitions, however, are not conceived in a true three-dimensional space. Thus we need to ask how an online exhibition should be conceived to maximize the possibilities of online design and minimize the disadvantages of the online environment.

Additionally, for the most part, the typical library or archival online exhibition (or for that matter, most online exhibitions from even the largest and best-funded museums) cannot hope to compete with the enhanced and interactive websites created by the likes of Disney, AOL/Time-Warner, or other large, multimedia megacorporations.

Still, this does not mean that an online exhibition needs to be a dull, static collection of images presented in a strict, linear fashion. On the contrary, "the design of interfaces should be considered an art form, similar to a performance, where shifts of attention are orchestrated throughout the text—which has the commanding role—and the other elements of the play" (Pierroux). In an online exhibition, as in a gallery exhibition, it is the presentation that brings to life the intellectual content of the script and unleashes the potential dynamism of the objects.

Jan Hjorth (1978), in *How to Make a Rotten Exhibition,* playfully lists a number of do's that make for a bad exhibition.

> The true designer must realize that it is the *exhibits* that count. Labels and other peripheral material are a secondary consideration. Better a slap-dash text than no text at all.
>
> One practical hint: long texts are often easier to write than short ones, apart from which they are more comprehensive and, ipso facto, more scientific.
>
> Always use scientifically accurate expressions, regardless of their intelligibility to the visitors.
>
> Pictures should be made both small and plentiful.
>
> Ignore all questions of copyright. Just take whatever you fancy in the way of pictures, photographs, drawings, and music.

In a more serious vein, Wendy Thomas and Danielle Boily (1998), in their "Virtual Exhibition Production: A Reference Guide," note a number of elements for a good online exhibition. These include

> Providing an opportunity to visit museum exhibitions more than once
>
> Allowing for surprise and wonder, and promoting dreaming and creation
>
> Giving an overall impression of the site on the home page
>
> Updating the site on a regular basis to attract visitors and keep them coming back
>
> Using source material provided by the medium to enhance meaning
>
> Displaying images that can be used on the Internet
>
> Designing the project like a research tool
>
> Providing access to normally inaccessible documents
>
> Ensuring research projects have international dissemination
>
> Hooking visitors by making browsing pleasant
>
> Touching users' emotions

Additionally, Bernadette G. Callery and Robert Thibadeau (2000) have asked a number of questions about what the design of an online exhibition should provide the viewer. Among the questions that they pose that could be solved through the creation of online exhibitions are

> Do museum visitors want to know more about exhibited objects?
>
> How can this additional information be organized and presented for the visitor's use?

What type of background and contextual information would the visitors select, such as correspondence or photographs, if given a choice?

How can archival documents be organized for presentation as an adjunct to an online exhibition?

How does online use of these adjunct archival materials differ from their on-site use, particularly in frequency of selection?

Do online visitors spend more time searching for and viewing this associated archival material than do on-site visitors?

The online environment neither excuses nor encourages bad exhibitions. It is up to the curators and designers of an online exhibition to be aware of its nature and take advantage of its unique opportunities to enhance the exhibition idea.

INTELLECTUAL PROPERTY ISSUES

"Ignore all questions of copyright. Just take whatever you fancy in the way of pictures, photographs, drawings, and music" is a bit of tongue-in-cheek advice quoted earlier from Jan Hjorth (1978). Needless to say, the willy-nilly appropriation of images, sounds, and video is unlikely to be condoned in many institutions (or by the institution's lawyers). More difficult to deal with is the use of intellectual property for which your library or archive has some claim.

As a general rule, it is best to clear all questions with the legal office of your institution. As with most moving targets, a written and closely adhered-to policy for use of materials, credits, and so forth will make your life easier.

If you will be using materials in your online exhibitions from other units of your institution or from unrelated institutions, be sure that you have a proper release form and credit clearance. The form you use may be similar to that used for print publication, with appropriate modifications.

In the rapidly changing arena of digital intellectual property law, it is important that you are as up-to-date as possible. For some examples of copyright and condition of use statements, see appendix C.

SOURCES CITED

Bearman, David. 1995. "Museum Strategies for Success on the Internet." Paper presented at Museum Collections and the Information Superhighway. Available at: http://www.mnsi.ac.uk/infosh/bearman.htm.

Belcher, Michael. 1991. *Exhibitions in Museums*. Washington, D.C.: Smithsonian Institution Press.

Bitgood, Stephen C. 1986. *Knowing When Exhibit Labels Work: A Standardized Guide for Evaluating and Improving Labels*. Jacksonville, Ala.: Jacksonville State University.

Callery, Bernadette G., and Robert Thibadeau. 2000. "On Beyond Label Copy: Museum-Library Collaboration in the Development of a Smart Web Exhibit." Paper presented at Museums and the Web: An International Conference. Available at: http://www.archimuse.com/mw2000/papers/callery/callery.html.

Dana, John Cotton. 1927. *Should Museums Be Useful?* Newark, N.J.: The Museum.

Goode, George Brown. 1891. "The Museums of the Future." In *Annual Report of the Board of Regents of the Smithsonian Institution for the Year Ending June 30, 1889*, pp. 427–445. Washington, D.C.: GPO.

Hjorth, Jan. 1978. *How to Make a Rotten Exhibition.* Stockholm: Riksutstallningar.

Horn, Emil. 1978. "Some Theoretical and Practical Questions of the Exhibitions of Recent and Contemporary History with Special Regard to the Permanent Exhibition of the Museum of the Hungarian Working Class Movement." In *The Problems of Contents, Didactics and Esthetics of Modern Museum Exhibitions*, ed. Ádám Szemere, pp. 107–127. Budapest: István Éri.

Pierroux, Palmyre. "Art in Networks: Information and Communication Technology in Art Museums." Available at: http://www.media.uio.no/internettiendring/publikasjoner/tekst/Pierroux/02Contents.html.

Serrell, Beverly. 1982. *Making Exhibit Labels: A Step-by-Step Guide.* Nashville: American Association for State and Local History.

———. 1998. *Paying Attention: Visitors and Museum Exhibitions.* Washington, D.C.: American Association of Museums.

Thomas, Wendy, and Danielle Boily. 1998. "Virtual Exhibition Production: A Reference Guide." Paper delivered at Museums and the Web: An International Conference. Available at: http://www.archimuse.com/mw98/papers/boily/boily_paper.html.

ONLINE EXHIBITIONS DISCUSSED

Daughter of Earth: Agnes Smedley and Smedley-MacKinnon Collections. Department of Archives and Manuscripts, Arizona State University Libraries.
http://www.asu.edu/lib/archives/smedley.htm

From Smithson to Smithsonian. Smithsonian Institution Libraries.
http://www.sil.si.edu/Exhibitions/Smithson-to-Smithsonian

Frontier Photographer: Edward S. Curtis. Smithsonian Institution Libraries.
http://www.sil.si.edu/Exhibitions/Curtis

Frontiers, Frontières, Fronteras: René Derouin. Glenbow Museum, Art Gallery, Library, and Archives.
http://www.glenbow.org/derouin/index.htm

A Great Assemblage. Yale University Library.
http://www.library.yale.edu/exhibition/judaica

John Bull and Uncle Sam: Four Centuries of British-American Relations. Library of Congress and British Library.
http://lcweb.loc.gov/exhibits/british

"Make the Dirt Fly!" Smithsonian Institution Libraries.
   http://www.sil.si.edu/Exhibitions/Make-the-Dirt-Fly

The Many Talents of John Gorham Palfrey, Our First Dean. Andover-Harvard
   Theological Library.
   http://www.hds.harvard.edu/library/exhibita/index.html

Nos Los Inquisidores. Department of Special Collections of the University
   Libraries of Notre Dame.
   http://www.rarebooks.nd.edu/Exbt/Inquisition

Out of This World: Canadian Science Fiction and Fantasy. National Library of
   Canada.
   http://www.nlc-bnc.ca/events/sci-fi/esci-fi.htm

Oveta Culp Hobby, the Little Colonel. Woodson Research Center, Special
   Collections at Fondren Library, Rice University.
   http://www.rice.edu/Fondren/Woodson/exhibits/wac

Recent Acquisitions in NCSU Libraries' Special Collections, 1998–1999. North
   Carolina State University.
   http://www.lib.ncsu.edu/archives/exhibits/newbooks99

Reflections in Time. Middle Tennessee State University.
   http://janus.mtsu.edu/Reflections/index.html

*The Romanovs: Their Empire, Their Books. The Political, Religious, Cultural, and
   Social Life of Russia's Imperial House.* New York Public Library.
   http://www.nypl.org/research/chss/slv/exhibit/roman.html

Rum, Riot, and Reform: Maine and the History of American Drinking. Maine
   Historical Society.
   http://www.mainehistory.org/rrr.html

Science and the Artist's Book. Smithsonian Institution Libraries.
   http://www.sil.si.edu/Exhibitions/Science-and-the-Artists-Book

Walt Whitman and the Development of "Leaves of Grass." University of South
   Carolina Libraries, Department of Rare Books and Special Collections.
   http://www.sc.edu/library/spcoll/amlit/whitman.html

The Writings of Paul Laurence Dunbar. Springfield Library, Rare Book and
   Special Collections.
   http://www.springfieldlibrary.org/dunbar/dunbar.html

CHAPTER 4

The Staff

In this chapter, the various roles of those responsible for an online exhibition will be outlined. Though in some cases each role will be carried out by a separate individual, in most libraries and archives, various aspects of the roles will be combined and executed by a smaller number of staff. The important thing to remember is that each of the roles is important and that each should be carried out by the individual best suited for that activity.

Just as in a gallery exhibition, tasks such as intellectual intent, organization, display planning, graphic design, and installation are devolved onto different persons or parts of an organization, so too with an online exhibition. At the same time, the online exhibition, no less so than one that graces an exhibition gallery, should bring together the talents of a group of people to best highlight the work on display.

STAFF FOR THE EXHIBITION

The following positions will be involved with an online exhibition:

Library or archive director	Editor
Curator	Education consultant
Designer	Production staff
Technical staff	Other
Conservator	

As previously noted, the same staff members may fill a number of these roles. Also, do not forget that in addition to your regular staff, your volunteers, interns, and student help can participate in the online exhibition process. The latter group will often be able to provide you with valuable talents and fresh outlooks on your exhibition projects.

Library or Archive Director

As with any activity at your library or archive, the overall responsibility for all functions ultimately rests with the director. The level of involvement that the director takes in online exhibitions will depend on his or her overall involvement with many of the day-to-day activities of the institution. Generally speaking, however, approval of the concept for the exhibition, the staff time, and any expenses will probably need to be cleared through the director.

Curator

As mentioned earlier, all exhibitions begin with an idea. But who is going to have the idea and who is going to carry through on the idea? In the museum world, the person in charge of a collection is the curator (a term we in library-land often apply to our rare book or special collections librarians). Curator, from the Latin *curator,* meaning "one who takes care of," implies a certain care and feeding of a group of objects. In fact, in Britain, the term *keeper* (as in Keeper of Antiquities at the British Museum or Keeper of the Catalog of American Portraits at the Smithsonian's National Portrait Gallery) is often used in place of *curator.*

In a museum, in addition to caring for the collections, curators are also usually responsible for displaying the objects in coherent and informative or educational ways. As Palmyre Pierroux in "Art in Networks: Information and Communication Technology in Art Museums" has noted, in web exhibitions, "a curator's interpretation may theoretically be accompanied by links to other sites—perhaps different viewpoints—and is often considered as empowering the museum visitor, stirring interest about a subject and enabling him/her to choose and configure the types of knowledge deemed relevant."

The curator for the exhibition is the person (or in some cases, a team of people) that is responsible for the overall intellectual content of the exhibition. At the same time, as Edward P. Alexander (1979, 189) notes, a "designer can keep an exhibit from becoming mediocre and stodgy, but a curator must see that it retains its truthfulness and sincerity."

Designer

In a gallery exhibition, the designer has a wide range of responsibilities that often includes the building skills necessary to create an installation in the exhibition space. The key role of the designer is to translate the concepts and ideas brought to the exhibition by the curator into a real physical space. Larry Klein (1986, 8) notes in *Exhibits: Planning and Design* that designers "are people who come to this work with an orientation to the spatial, visual, and concrete aspects of our world. They bring a sense of relationships and of the taste and smell of things."

In an online exhibition, the designer will have many of the same responsibilities for the look and feel of the exhibition (including such things as choosing thematic colors and image motifs). The designer of an online exhibition will need to work with the tools and skill sets of the web designer to supplement those of a gallery exhibition designer. As in a gallery exhibition, the designer will work closely with the curator (and in some cases will be the curator) so that the ideas underlying the exhibition are translated to the screen.

Designing and envisioning a web exhibition should be significantly different from designing a gallery exhibition. In the gallery experience, the viewer is able to grasp a large portion of the designer's vision in a glance across the gallery space. With an online exhibition, though general design elements will be immediately apprehensible, significant portions of the exhibition will only reveal themselves slowly to the viewer.

General skills to look for in a designer include knowledge of the tools and practices of good web design, the ability to take a design through various stages of development as modifications to the original idea are made by the curator, and, most importantly, the ability to conceptualize a design based on the exhibition idea.

In wall space, museum cases, or vitrines, a designer is able to present objects full size or even, in the case of wall graphics, enlarged and enhanced. The web designer, however, is limited by technical constraints (e.g., screen size) that will inform his or her design. At the same time, the online exhibition designer can take advantage of the Web's interactive nature to allow the viewer to explore many objects in more detail than is available in a gallery space.

Technical Staff

In a gallery exhibition, the technical staff may be the carpenters and painters, the case builders, and the printers who put the show together. For an online exhibition, a technical staff will also be necessary. As online exhibitions become more complex and take advantage of more and more whizbang Internet tools, the skill sets of the exhibition designer and technical staff will grow. Database development, web-database integration, CGI (Common Gateway Interface) script writing, Perl programming, scanning, and photography are just a few of the skills that may be required of the technical staff for an online exhibition.

Conservator

Depending upon the nature of an online exhibition, consultation with the preservation/conservation staff may be necessary to determine if (and how) the items can be digitized or photographed. Integrating online exhibitions into the work flow of your conservation staff will be a workload issue that will need to be carefully considered when planning for online exhibitions.

Editor

Even the most perfect of us makes an occasional typo or confuses entomology with etymology. A second (or third or fourth) pair of eyes to proof all the text and information embedded in the images of an online exhibition is key. The editor of the exhibition should have a thorough knowledge of correct grammar, writing styles, and sentence construction. Additionally, the editor should be able to analyze, organize, and rewrite the exhibition text as needed for clarity.

Another important task that you may wish to assign to the editorial position is rights clearance and copyright compliance. If you are using objects that are lent from other institutions or other parts of your own institution, you will most likely need to get clearance for their use. Likewise, before you mount digital representations of objects in your own collection, it is always a good idea to make certain that there are no limitations of copyright or licensing that will cause problems.

Education Consultant

The main purpose of an exhibition education consultant is to provide a wider range of learning experiences for the viewers of the exhibition. To this end, various supplemental products can be created for your online exhibition. These products can range from lesson plans for teachers to targeted reading lists for selected age groups.

If you work in an institution that offers education degrees, you may be able to enlist students from those programs to create education components for your exhibitions. Others may seek help from the local education community or even hire an education consultant. No matter which path is taken, skills to look for in an education consultant include a knowledge of exhibition education techniques, a general knowledge of the topic of the exhibition, an ability to design an education program, and an ability to work with the curator and design staff.

Production Staff

Depending upon how you plan to digitize your objects, staff will need to be assigned to the process. If slides are being used, digitization will be a fairly simple procedure; if, however, you will need to have new slides shot or use a more complex digitization laboratory (e.g., a scanning back or an orbital digital camera), production staff can either do the work themselves or act as the intermediaries for scheduling and so forth.

Other Staff

Other staff to handle such elements of the exhibition as publicity and translation (if you wish to mount the site in more than one language) may be needed. Additionally, for larger-scale exhibitions that may entail significant funding, a staff person to coordinate development efforts will be needed. And, as always, you may wish to consult with legal staff about such issues as copyright.

BUILDING A TEAM

Once your curator has his or her exhibition idea in place, it is time to assemble the team that will bring the idea to the online world. How the online exhibition team works together will depend on a number of factors, including the size of the exhibition, the number of people involved in producing it, and the overall working environment of your library or archive.

For the sake of elucidating the concept of team building, let's assume that for your online exhibition the various roles will be filled by individual staff members. After the initial approval of the exhibition by the administrative unit of the library or archive, the curator can start the research and investigation necessary to begin preparing the exhibition. In most cases, the curator will do most of the preparation for the exhibition by him- or herself and then begin to assemble the team. As the objects for the exhibition are selected, a meeting of all the players involved with the exhibition should be held to determine schedules and the roles that will be played. As Wendy Thomas and Danielle Boily (1998) note, one of the first lessons to learn is "the importance of allowing sufficient time for the participants to become acquainted and develop the sense of being part of a team."

It is important that timelines, specific roles, and clear lines of communication be set up early in the exhibition planning. Duplication of effort or, more likely, missed deadlines and lost steps can easily derail an exhibition.

The Staff

INTEGRATING EXHIBITIONS INTO STAFF ACTIVITIES

Online exhibitions do not have to be special projects, created and organized by only selected staff members. One goal of an online exhibition program should be to integrate elements of online exhibitions into the regular work environment. As mentioned above, many of the regular activities of staff can be the focus of an online exhibition, and staff should be encouraged to see in what ways their work can contribute to online exhibitions. For example, when exhibitions are integrated into staff work, the cataloging staff would supply metadata for the online exhibition (to increase the ease of finding it in online search engines) as well as provide a catalog record for the online catalog, and reference staff would assist the curator with bibliographies or webliographies.

SOURCES CITED

Alexander, Edward P. 1979. *Museums in Motion*. Nashville: American Association for State and Local History.

Glaser, Jane R., and Artemis A. Zenetou. 1996. *Museums: A Place to Work. Planning Museum Careers*. London and New York: Routledge.

Goode, George Brown. 1891. "The Museums of the Future." In *Annual Report of the Board of Regents of the Smithsonian Institution for the Year Ending June 30, 1889,* pp. 427–445. Washington, D.C.: GPO.

Klein, Larry. 1986. *Exhibits: Planning and Design*. New York: Madison Square.

Pierroux, Palmyre. "Art in Networks: Information and Communication Technology in Art Museums." Available at: http://www.media.uio.no/internettiendring/publikasjoner/tekst/Pierroux/02Contents.html.

Thomas, Wendy, and Danielle Boily. 1998. "Virtual Exhibition Production: A Reference Guide." Museums and the Web: An International Conference. Available at: http://www.archimuse.com/mw98/papers/boily/boily_paper.html.

Technical Issues
Digitizing

Even the most perfect reproduction of a work of art is lacking in one element: its presence in time and space, its unique existence at the place where it happens to be. . . . Technical reproduction can put the copy of the original into situations which would be out of reach for the original itself. Above all, it enables the original to meet the beholder halfway.

—Walter Benjamin

Why are we only now getting to the technical issues? Just tell me how to scan an object, write an HTML page, and slap it on a web server. The other stuff is the easy part. I need to know what the geeks know to have a great online exhibition!

These days anybody can scan a slide (or have photo developers do it), write an HTML page (or use a word processor to create what passes in some circles for HTML), choose from dozens of free point-and-click web-hosting services, and voilà, an instant website. Well, I hope the preceding chapters have convinced you that this notion is as wrong as wrong can be. In part, anyway! In this chapter, we will go over some of the basics for creating digital content, file formats, and what you can do to help preserve your digital, online exhibition.

DIGITIZING METHODS

Images

First, let's start with a quick overview of the ways in which you can acquire digital images. For the purposes of an online exhibition, there are basically four options:

Scanning back camera	Flatbed scanner
Digital camera	Slide scanner

A fifth option, that of creating the image from scratch using a graphic illustration program such as Adobe Illustrator, is not relevant for converting objects to digital form.

Scanning Back Camera.   A digital scanning back camera is at the high end of digitization options. A scanning back camera is similar in appearance to a regular analog photographic camera. In place of a film back, however, is an optical array similar to the array on a flatbed scanner. The camera is mounted on a fixed camera stand with lights and other equipment such as you would find on a camera copy stand to complete the setup. You will also need a computer (probably a Mac) to run the camera. The pros of a scanning back camera are the high quality of the images you can create and the strong control you have over the setup of a book or manuscript object. The primary drawbacks to the scanning back camera are its cost and the skill level needed to operate it. A complete package (camera, scanning back, copy stand, computer, and so forth) can cost upward of $75,000. It is unlikely that any archives or library will invest this much money simply to create online exhibitions. It is possible, however, that such a setup is in use for other digitizing initiatives at your institution and that objects for online exhibitions can be slipped into the work flow of a digitizing center.

Digital Camera.   Simple snapshot digital cameras are rapidly dropping in price, and low-end models can be had for well under $200. The quality of the low-end (and even mid- to high-end) digital cameras, however, is not suitable for the type of detail required for good-quality online exhibitions (except perhaps for certain object-type shots that you may wish to use to supplement the exhibition). Lack of fine focus, lighting, and other shortcomings do not make the current digital cameras viable options for use in online exhibitions.

Flatbed Scanner.   The quality of imaging you will get from a flatbed scanner makes it an excellent choice for some of the work for an online exhibition. As we know from years of experience with photocopiers, however, such machines can destroy even the best of commercial bindings. The primary drawback of a flatbed scanner is that it cannot safely handle many of our materials, especially bound books and manuscripts that may be damaged by the handling required to place them facedown for digitizing. Scanners are increasingly affordable, and even scanners capable of handling large-format materials are available for under $500.

Slide Scanner.   In many ways, a slide scanner is the easiest, cheapest, and best solution to the digitizing needs of online exhibitions. It enables you to digitize quality 35-millimeter slides of your books, manuscripts, and other objects. Many libraries and archives already have staff trained in handling materials and the use of a camera copy stand and lights. Teams composed of material handlers and photographers can work together to make the best possible 35-millimeter images of the objects in the exhibition. Scanning the slides is then a fairly straightforward proposition. Though the quality of the resultant images is entirely dependent upon the quality of the original slides, a slide scanner should provide serviceable images for online exhibition purposes. Suitable slide scanners are available for between $400 and $800.

In many situations, it is likely that you will be using a mix of scanning equipment for the objects in your online exhibition. Take advantage of the equipment and expertise you have at hand to make the best possible images for your exhibitions.

DIGITIZING STANDARDS FOR ONLINE EXHIBITIONS

Images

Once you have selected a digitizing method for your objects, you should settle upon a set of standards for the objects in that exhibition. First, however, a few definitions of terms might come in handy:

Dots per inch (dpi) is the measurement used to describe the resolution of an image. The more dots per inch, the higher the resolution.

Color depth refers to the number of colors available in an image. Table 1 shows the common color-depth options.

Image size may refer to the linear measurements of an original object, the size of an image in kilobytes (i.e., its file space requirements), or the height and length of an image in pixels. Table 2 shows the different image sizes (in kilobytes and pixels) and the same object scanned at different settings.

Before that first image capture, plan the imaging standards you will use for the project. Some elements of the project standards will include:

Technical specifications of the equipment you are using (you cannot scan at 600 dpi if your scanner has a capacity for only 400 dpi)

Additional uses for the images created (e.g., print use, 300 to 600 dpi)

Time available for digitizing (higher dpi's generally result in longer scan times)

Storage plans for the images (larger images will take more storage space)

TABLE 1 Color Bit Depth Chart

Bit Depth	Exponential Expression	Colors Available
1 bit	2^1	2 colors (black and white)
4 bit	2^4	16 colors
8 bit	2^8	256 colors
16 bit	2^{16}	Thousands of colors
24 bit	2^{24}	Millions of colors
36 bit	2^{36}	Billions of colors

TABLE 2 Scanned Image Sizes

Input Size (in inches)	DPI	% of Original Image Size	Color Depth	Output Size (in inches)	File Size (kilobytes)	Pixel Size (approx.)
5.5 × 4	300	100	24 bit	5.5 × 4	5,904	1,644 × 1,215
5.5 × 4	300	200	24 bit	11 × 8	5,904	3,510 × 2,354
5.5 × 4	300	100	36 bit	5.5 × 4	11,808	1,644 × 1,215
5.5 × 4	100	100	24 bit	5.5 × 4	657	548 × 405
5.5 × 4	100	600	24 bit	33 × 24	23,619	3,288 × 2,430
5.5 × 4	300	50	24 bit	2.75 × 2	1,477	823 × 608

As a general rule, you should always scan at the highest practical level. You will be making lower-resolution images (often called derivative images) from these high-level scans. Once you have digitized an object, you do not want to go back and handle it again if possible. Table 3 lists suggested scanning specifications for different types of equipment.

By looking at table 2, you can see that scanning at a very high dpi, at a large percentage of the original image, and at a high color depth will result in a file that is large both in actual size (i.e., inches or pixels) and in byte size. Note the significant difference in scanning an image at 100 dpi and 300 dpi, both at 100 percent of the original. The smaller dpi results in an image that is only 548 by 405 pixels. Though this is a nice size for mounting on a website, if you wanted to enlarge the image or a portion of it, you would quickly begin to lose detail. This same image at 300 dpi results in an image 1,644 by 1,215 pixels. This size will give you plenty of leeway for cropping and enlarging portions of the image.

Also note that the output size for an image can be greatly increased by controlling the dpi and the percentage of the original image. Though less relevant for the online exhibition aspect of the scanning, this factor can be important if you ever need to use the image in a print publication. Again, generally speaking, you will want a minimum of 300 dpi for any image that will later be used in a print medium.

Choosing between 24- and 36-bit color when digitizing strictly for online presentation is not that important. As you can see from table 2, the inflated size of the file created with 36-bit color outweighs any slight perceptual difference that may occur. Of course, if you are scanning for other purposes (and have the extra time and plenty of storage space), by all means go ahead and take full advantage of your scanning capability.

In table 3 you will note that for slide scanning, a much higher resolution is suggested. As your original image size for slides will be only 35 millimeters, your original image is relatively small. Using a higher dpi for scanning will thus give you a nice size image to work with or to enlarge for other purposes.

Image Quality Control

The first phase of quality control occurs at the time an image is captured. As a general rule, you should check for the following when you are previewing the scan of an object:

Alignment   Cropping   Exposure

If you are scanning large amounts of material in a batch mode (or if the scanning is being done by volunteer, student, or other nonregular scanning

TABLE 3 Scanning Specifications

Equipment	DPI	Color Depth	Image Size
Scanning Back Camera	300–600	36 bit	100% of original
Digital Camera	N/A	24–36 bit	100% of original
Flatbed Scanner	300–600	36 bit	100% of original
Slide Scanner	2,400	36 bit	100% of original

staff), you will want the scanners to check images regularly (approximately every third to fifth image) for

Sharp focus	Skewing of image	Color accuracy

Before the final launch of the exhibition (and, one would hope, well earlier), you will want to perform a quality review process. The first quality review occurs after images have been created and the primary derivatives have been created. This should leave you time to correct any mistakes before going live. When you review a batch of derivatives, give each one a pass/fail rating. Images are failed if

Typeface or ink lines are obviously blurry.

The exposure is obviously wrong—too light or too dark (compare the test image against others from the same item if you're not sure).

The page is obviously skewed.

The image is not at the same resolution or physical size as prescribed by the scanning instructions.

COMMON IMAGE FILE FORMATS

Now that you've captured your image, how are you going to save it? There are literally dozens of potential file formats that can be used to save images. Let's go through a number of the more common ones and the ones you will most likely see in an online environment.

Graphical Interchange Format (GIF)

The Graphical Interchange Format (pronounced either "jiff" or "g-if") was introduced in the 1980s by Compuserv to allow the transfer of files on its proprietary network. GIF soon became one of the most common image file formats and, for a time, was the only format supported by the Mosaic web browser (my, how times change!).

GIF is more limited in its handling of colors, providing support for only 256 colors. Additionally, the inability of GIF to handle gamma will make images appear brighter on Windows machines and dimmer on Macs, and vice versa. Though still useful for images that use large swaths of color (such as logos), it is less useful for images of objects. Another popular use of GIF is for animated images.

Though there has been some debate on the licensing of GIF, the controversy is primarily of concern to software developers and not to creators of images in GIF.

Joint Photographic Experts Group (JPEG)

JPEG (pronounced "jay-peg") is a standardized image-compression mechanism. JPEG stands for Joint Photographic Experts Group, the group that wrote the standard. JPEG is useful for creating full-color or grayscale images of natural, real-world scenes. It works well on photographs or as an output of scanned objects.

JPEG is "lossy," which means that when an image is saved in the JPEG format, some of the data is lost in the compression. By saving at different compression levels, smaller or larger images (with corresponding loss of quality or sharpness) will result.

Tag Image File Format (TIFF)	The Tag Image File Format (note "tag," not "tagged") was originally developed by Aldus Corporation (which eventually became Adobe). TIFF files are capable of storing all types of images (bilevel, grayscale, palette-color, and full-color image data in several color spaces). TIFF also allows for a number of different compression schemes.
Portable Network Graphics (PNG)	The Portable Network Graphics (PNG) format (pronounced "ping") was designed to replace the older and simpler GIF format and, to some extent, the TIFF format. For use on the Web, PNG is more effective for controlling image brightness as well as providing variable transparency for images. It also has the ability, like the JPEG format, to provide interlacing (a progressive image display that allows part of an image to display while the rest is downloading). PNG images can be compressed more than GIFs, but not as much as JPEGs. As a TIFF replacement, PNG provides a lossless compression (unlike JPEG).
Photoshop File Format (PSD)	The native format for Photoshop files, the PSD format allows the user to save features such as layers and undo in created files. The Paintshop Pro equivalent is PSP.
Kodak Photo CD (PCD)	The Photo CD (PCD) format is a proprietary format developed by Eastman Kodak to store digitized photographic images on CD-ROM discs. The Photo CD format allows for storing multiple image resolutions in a single file (e.g., 192 by 128 pixels, 384 by 256 pixels, 768 by 512 pixels, 1,536 by 1,024 pixels, and 3,072 by 2,048 pixels).

TABLE 4 Summary of Image File Format Types

Filetype Name	Common Extension	Typical Usage
Graphical Interchange Format	.gif	Graphics with large swaths of single colors; animated images
Joint Photographic Experts Group	.jpg or .jpeg	Web-deliverable images; working copies of images
Tag Image File Format	.tif	Common format to capture images; archival image storage format
Portable Network Graphics	.png	Designed to replace GIF and (partially) TIFF, useful for general web-image work
Photoshop File Format	.psd	The native Photoshop format; useful for saving stages of manipulating and editing images
Kodak Photo CD	.pcd	Acceptable for image storage

DERIVATIVES AND IMAGES FOR WEB DISPLAY

Many of the file formats described above will be useful for some parts of the production of your online exhibitions. The PNG format is gaining acceptance as a replacement for the GIF format. Either of those file formats is suitable for thumbnails. For most production it is recommended that you use TIFF (for capture and storage) and JPEG (for web-deliverables).

TIFF Images

All images should be saved as uncompressed TIFF files. TIFF files will allow you to further manipulate the images without loss of image quality if you ever need them for other purposes. If you use color or grayscale bars in the capture of your objects, your TIFF files will take up quite a bit of space. Thus, you will want to save them to an appropriate archival CD-ROM for longer-term storage (unless you have plenty of network space for image storage). The TIFF, scanned and saved at a high resolution, can come in handy for other uses (such as print products).

First JPEGs

Save a working copy of each image as a large JPEG image. This image will be the same as your TIFF, but saving it as a JPEG file will greatly reduce the size of the file and the time needed to manipulate it. You will want to save this at the minimum compression level available with your imaging software and at the original scanning dpi. Save the file at Photoshop quality level 10/12.

Web-Deliverable Images

For your exhibition, you will need to create web-deliverable images. Depending on the nature of your exhibition and the design, you may create a number of web-deliverables for each object in the exhibition. These could include full-size images, thumbnail images, and enlargements of portions of the objects. These images are cropped, de-skewed, and rotated. Each image is resized according to project/item plans (discussed below). Also, since these images are designed for viewing on the Web, you should reduce each to between 72 and 75 dpi to create a smaller file. Generally these files will be in the JPEG format at Photoshop quality level 7 (high).

From the first JPEGs, the following web-deliverable images may be created:

Full-Size Images. In most cases, you will want to give visitors to your online exhibition a large image of each of the objects. Though in your text you may include only thumbnails or midsize images (see below), a hypertext link will allow visitors to see the images as large as you like. It is suggested that full-size images be created at the following sizes:

> For portrait-oriented images, 650 pixels on the top (or short side) with a proportionally scaled length (or long side)

> For landscape-oriented images, 1,000 pixels on the top (or long side) with a proportionally scaled length (or short side)

Depending on your design, you may also wish to put a three- to five-pixel border around the image in a color that matches or complements your design scheme (black is also always a good choice). It is in this image that you may want to put identifying information (author, title, copyright statement, credit lines, and so forth). This text can be embedded in a highly contrasting color to the border (such as white). For landscape-oriented images, the top or bottom borders can be increased in size to accommodate this text. For portrait-oriented images, it is often more practical (though somewhat inconvenient for the viewer) to extend the right or left borders and run the text vertically.

Midsize Images. The pixel size of a midsize image will depend upon its use. Uses of borders and text will be a factor in how midsize images are used in the design.

Thumbnails. The pixel size of a thumbnail image will depend upon its use. Uses of borders and text will influence how thumbnails are used in the design. Generally, a thumbnail will be no larger than 150 pixels on the top (short) side of a portrait-oriented image and 250 pixels on the top (long) side of a landscape-oriented image.

For some of the best advice on creating images for the Web, see the work of Lynda Weinman. Her books *Designing Web Graphics.3* and *Deconstructing Web Graphics* and her website (http://www.lynda.com) are great helps.

OTHER MEDIA FILE FORMATS

Though the Web offers the opportunity to supplement your online exhibition with multimedia, be fully aware of the pros and cons of filling your exhibition with too many whizbang effects. Among the excuses for using multimedia (some more valid than others) are

> Many visitors will expect the latest bells, whistles, and flying monkeys on your site.
>
> You can do it.
>
> You just paid (fill in the amount) for some new software and want to play with it.
>
> Some media (e.g., audio) may be more accessible to some users.

Among the disadvantages are

> Many visitors (especially those with low bandwidth or older web browsers) will be annoyed by the latest bells, whistles, and flying monkeys on your site.
>
> Memo to hammer owners: not all problems are nails; just because you can doesn't mean you should.
>
> You don't have (fill in the dollar amount) for some new software and don't have time to play with it anyway.
>
> Some media (e.g., audio) may be less accessible to some users.

For online exhibitions, you may offer audio and video clips that will supplement the images in your exhibition.

HOLD ONTO THOSE PIXELS!

Standards, Dewey decimals, archives, longevity. These are not sexy topics, but unless we pay attention, history may end up being understood by our grandchildren in a much different way than we lived it.—Steve Dietz

Preservation of digital media is both a hot topic and one for which most answers are unavailable. For online exhibitions, the best bet for now is to make sure your imaging work is done at the highest level practical. Save your images as TIFFs and store them in a medium that is migratable. In most cases, the file backups that you do for your local area network or web server will be sufficient until your institution's long-term storage or archival solutions are in place. Another alternative is to transfer your exhibition TIFF images (as well as the entire content of the exhibition itself) to gold media CD-ROM. Keep two copies of the disks in separate locations as further disaster recovery insurance.

For a good discussion of issues relating to the preservation of digital media, see the *Handbook for Digital Projects: A Management Tool for Preservation and Access*, edited by Maxine K. Sitts (2000).

SOURCES CITED

Benjamin, Walter. 1969. "The Work of Art in the Age of Mechanical Reproduction." In *Illuminations*, ed. Hannah Arendt, pp. 217–251. New York: Schocken.

Dietz, Steve. 1998. "Curating (on) the Web in an Interface Culture." Available at: http://www.archimuse.com/mw98/papers/dietz/dietz_curatingtheweb.html.

Fulton, Wayne. A Few Scanning Tips. Available at: http://www.scantips.com.

Kenney, Anne R., and Louis H. Sharpe II. 1999. Illustrated Book Study: Digital Conversion Requirements Printed Illustrations. With Barbara Berger, Rick Crowhurst, D. Michael Ott, and Allen Quirk. Available at: http://www.lcweb.loc.gov/preserv/rt/illbk/ibs.htm.

Sitts, Maxine K., ed. 2000. *Handbook for Digital Projects: A Management Tool for Preservation and Access.* Andover, Mass.: Northeast Document Conservation Center. Available at: http://www.nedcc.org/digital/dighome.htm.

Weinman, Lynda. 1998. *Deconstructing Web Graphics*. Indianapolis: New Riders.

——. 1999. *Designing Web Graphics.3.* Indianapolis: New Riders.

SOURCES OF INFORMATION ON FILE FORMATS

General

Chamberlain, Bryan. Understanding Image File Formats. Available at: http://www.elementkjournals.com/tma/9508/tma95801.htm.

Image FAQ. Available at: http://www.oreilly.com/centers/gff/gff-faq/gff-faq1.htm.

GIF

Graphics Interchange Format. Available at: ftp.ncsa.uiuc.edu:/misc/file.formats/graphics.formats/gif87a.doc.

JPEG

JPEG FAQ. Available at: http://www.faqs.org/faqs/jpeg-faq.

PNG

JPEG FAQ. Available at: http://www.faqs.org/faqs/jpeg-faq.

Just PNG. Available at: http://www.freesoftware.com/pub/png.

Tag Image File Format

RFC 2302 Tag Image File Format (TIFF). Available at: http://www.kblabs.
com/lab/lib/rfcs/2300/rfc2302.txt.html.

Audio

How to Digitize Audio for Playback through a Computer. Available at:
http://www.jhepple.com/Freestuff/how_to_digitize_audio.htm.

Pohlmann, Ken C. 2000. *Principles of Digital Audio.* New York: McGraw-Hill.

Video

How to Digitize Video. Available at: http://www.geocities.com/
CapeCanaveral/Orbit/1038/howtodig.htm.

Technical Issues
Markup Languages

Entire online exhibitions do not appear on the Web just by magic! Behind each word, image, and sound clip lies a whole hidden world of markup tags, or codes, that create the layout and appearance of web pages and allow them to appear as their creator intends. For the Web, the basic language of markup tags is Hypertext Markup Language (HTML). The creation of Hypertext Markup Language created a miniboom in publishing that rivaled those created by the introduction of mimeograph and copy machines. The basic concepts and tag sets of HTML were easy enough to learn, and the handy "reveal codes" feature of web browsers enabled the rest of us to borrow the markup of pages we liked to get just the right look. For most online exhibitions being created today, HTML, or its newest replacement, XHTML (about which more later), will be the markup language of choice. How much you need to know about markup languages will depend upon your level of interest as well as the specific tools that you will use when creating an online exhibition. A little background on how we got to HTML (and XHTML) might be of some use to newer web writers. However, this chapter will not be an HTML primer. See the many suggested resources for more detailed instruction in page markup.

STANDARD GENERALIZED MARKUP LANGUAGE (SGML)

It has been waggishly noted that Standard Generalized Markup Language (SGML) is neither standard, generalized, nor a markup language. Be that as it may, SGML, or "ISO 8879:1986. Information processing—Text and office systems—Standard Generalized Markup Language (SGML)," has become an indispensable tool for structuring and formatting documents. As a markup language, SGML is able to describe the document's content structure in a logical way and creates the ability to define what physical characteristics those elements possess (font, margins, spacing, and so forth).

For the Web, SGML has manifested itself in the form of HTML. HTML, the primary method of delivering documents via the Web, is simply an SGML document type definition (DTD; the SGML element that describes and provides a framework for the structure of the document) that pertains to the markup of HTTP-delivered documents. The current version of HTML, v.4.01 (24 December 1999), is not a standard of its own but rather a DTD of SGML.

HYPERTEXT MARKUP LANGUAGE (HTML)

First, a little background. HTML is a markup language designed to display text on a screen and provide hypertext links to other documents. Early versions of HTML were limited in their ability to create screen layouts that approach the functionality of the printed page. Later versions of HTML added elements, such as the <table> tag, the align element, the <font> tag, and others that made screen layout slightly more attractive.

HTML documents began appearing in 1991, shortly after the creation of the HyperText Transfer Protocol (HTTP). With the introduction of the Graphical User Interface (GUI) web browser Mosaic in early 1993, the potential of using the World Wide Web for Internet delivery of a range of documents and projects dawned on a host of Net users.

Version 3.2 of HTML is considered by many to be the final word in the HTML standard. However, in mid-1997 work was begun on HTML 4.0, which would incorporate even more of the special tags used by web browsers such as Netscape and Internet Explorer. Among the more controversial tags HTML 4.0 accepted was the <frame> tag that allowed multiple navigable pages to appear on the user's screen. HTML 4.0 also standardized the use of scripts, more fully supported style sheets, and made documents more accessible to users with disabilities. The earliest codified version of HTML 4.0 appeared in late 1997, and minor revisions continued on the document until late 1999, when HTML 4.01 was released.

DYNAMIC HTML (DHTML)

Dynamic HTML, which builds on the work done for the HTML 4.01 standard, is nothing more than that most dreaded of beasts, the paradigm shift. No official standard for DHTML exists, but rather, a host of concepts and technologies work together within the HTML 4.01 environment to create pages that the user can interact with after the page has loaded into the client, with no need to call on the server again.

The key components of DHTML are the standards and tags developed for HTML 4.01. Additional elements include the use of special scripting language (such as JavaScript, more about which in chapter 7) and style sheets.

So, will DHTML solve all the problems of web development, bring better structured documents to the Web, help me find all the information I want, and give whiter, brighter teeth? Sadly, no. HTML (even the DHTML flavor) has become so encumbered with nonstandard tags that developers feel it's just as well to stop adding elements and start from scratch—or if not quite from scratch, to go back to SGML and create a markup language that can meet the needs of more complex web documents. But don't give up hope! Style sheets and newer markup languages will rescue us.

CASCADING STYLE SHEETS (CSS)

Style sheets, and specifically cascading style sheets (CSS), are a component of markup languages that allow the page creator to more accurately and easily control the layout and look and feel of a web page. You may not have noticed, but the Web is not really WYSIWYG (what you see is what you get). The page you just designed, the new exhibition that just went live, those wonderful works of web art you just created just do not look as impressive to your friends down at the cybercafé as they did on your PC at work. What happened to all your layout? The carefully constructed columns and the special fonts you used? The indentation and alignment of all those paragraphs of text?

Returning to your cubical, you go back to the drawing board (or your trusty HTML editor) and start to torture your <table> tags until things look a bit better. But that's not enough! To make certain that all your favorite fonts appear in just the size and positioning you want, you drop the whole text charade and load your pages with bit-mapped images of words that may take longer to download but will, if you're lucky, look more or less (well, maybe a little less than more) the same on every monitor in the world.

Yeah, you know that no one ever promised that HTML would replace desktop publishing programs like Quark, but, well, you had hopes. And now, those hopes are a little closer to fulfillment. What is it that brings us just a tad closer to desktop publishing on the Web? Nothing other than cascading style sheets.

HTML versus the Page Designer

Creative web page designers integrated bit-mapped text images, pixel shims (or clear GIFs), and resized one-by-one-pixel points of color to achieve remarkable results. All too often, however, these results didn't port to other browsers or screen resolutions. Bit-mapped text images sometimes shrank (or grew) in odd ways, depending on the viewer's screen resolution, and pixel shims did the same when used to create fixed-width table cells. All the elements of HTML that were created primarily to define document structure (e.g., all the heading tags such as <h1>) were shanghaied into acting as display elements.

Elements of Style

What the web page designer really needs is a way to control all the elements of the page layout or, at a minimum, to control the variations that might occur. Even better would be a way to control those elements for a large number of web pages without having to change each page if a change in font size or color is made—in short, a style sheet that could be applied across a site. Style sheets for the Web were first proposed by Håkon W. Lie in late 1994. It wasn't until May 1996, however, that the web style sheet as we now know it was introduced by the World Wide Web Consortium (W3C) and implemented with Microsoft's Internet Explorer 3.0.

The basic concept behind the HTML style sheet is that the page creator can define how certain formatting tags and elements will appear. Those definitions can be applied in any of three ways: locally (also called inline), globally (or embedded), or as linked definitions.

In a local definition, each tag is defined each time it is used. Thus, instead of <h2> using the browser's defaults, the page creator could define the <h2> tag as follows:

```
<h2 style=font-size: 35pt; color: red; font-family:
"Verdana, Arial, Helvetica">
```

In a global style sheet, the definitions are made in the head of the document. Thus:

```
<html>

<head>

<style type="text/css">
```

```
<!—

h4 {font: 17pt "Arial, Helvetica"; color: green}

h2 {font: 15pt "Arial, Helvetica"; color: blue}

p {font: 12pt "Arial, Helvetica";}

—>

</style>

</head>

<body>

        . . .

</body>

</html>
```

Any text not covered by the tags defined in the style sheet will be displayed as the browser default. The most powerful way to use the style sheet is to implement it as a linked style sheet. By creating a style sheet document (e.g., stylesheet.css) and referencing it on each page, global changes to any of a whole collection of pages that reference the style sheet can be made simply by changing the style sheet. The .css file itself will resemble the markup above, but without the enclosing HTML envelope tags:

```
h4 {font: 17pt "Arial, Helvetica"; color: green}

h2 {font: 15pt "Arial, Helvetica"; color: blue}

p {font: 12pt "Arial, Helvetica";}
```

To use this style sheet, simply save it as a file and then reference the file from each page to which you wish to apply the style. In the head of each page, add a link to the style sheet in the following format:

```
<head>

<link rel=stylesheet href="stylesheetname.css"

type="text/css">

</head>
```

By using all three types of style sheets (local, global, and linked), a page designer can have an amazing amount of control over the page layout. The notion of cascading comes in to describe the hierarchy of the style sheets. *Local* style sheets take precedence over *global* ones, and global style sheets take precedence over *linked* ones.

The User Agent

The true power imparted by style sheets is the ability to control page layout. This makes the page accessible to any number of style-sheet-compatible web browsers. More importantly, the flexibility of style sheets has generated a successor term for the browser: the *user agent*. Style sheets allow web content to be adapted to a range of tools the consumer of a web page might use: a traditional graphical or text-mode web browser, a Braille reader, a speech-synthesis tool, or simply a printer.

Although use of style sheets makes the web designer's job easier, it doesn't make a designer out of anyone who can master the elements of CSS. Another important point to remember is that CSS pages may not look as good on earlier-generation browsers (er, user agents) without careful thought and planning by the designer. Thus, the page that looks wonderful on your new model web browser may look totally different on your grandfather's version 3.0 of Netscape.

For online exhibitions, the use of style sheets will enable you to control the look of many pages and to make quick changes during the course of your design process.

XML: eXtensible Markup Language

So, just what is this latest markup language that's expected to hit all the web-sites and give web masters alternating feelings of power and helplessness? Nothing more than XML, or eXtensible Markup Language. Though approved as a standard way back in October 1998 (and lacking any full-blown applications), XML is only now starting to take the online world by storm.

XML is a markup language built from the start to be extensible, meaning that you, the creator, can make up any tags you like (as long as you specify them in your XML DTD). XML is designed to enable the use of SGML on the World Wide Web in a more robust manner than was ever possible with HTML. In November 1996, the first XML working draft was announced, and since that time the World Wide Web Consortium has taken on the responsibility of helping define the standard.

A very basic definition of XML is that it's a document type definition (DTD) of SGML for WWW delivery of information. You might even think of it as a dialect of SGML. But wait, you say, isn't that what HTML is? Yes, the key difference is that XML offers the following three benefits not found in HTML:

Extensibility. HTML does not allow users to specify their own tags or attributes in order to parameterize or otherwise semantically qualify their data.

Structure. HTML does not support the specification of deep structures needed to represent database schemas or object-oriented hierarchies.

Validation. HTML does not support the kind of language specification that allows consuming applications to check data for structural validity on importation.

Through a number of extensions—many of them browser-specific—HTML has been made to look like it can handle more complex format and structure elements than it really can. As noted in *HTML Unleashed:* "If we strip away for a moment the innumerable struts, crutches, and sophisticated gizmos that make the HTML golem walk and speak and look alive, what we'll see will be a pretty simple (not to say primitive) markup language designed for basic documents of a quite predictable structure."

XML, by allowing the page creator to define any number of tags (and how they will look and behave), avoids the problems of HTML. Another key element of XML is that it supports Unicode. XML employs ISO 10646, the international standard 31-bit character set that covers most human (and some nonhuman) written languages. XML documents (as well as the XML tags themselves) can be written in nearly any language.

Best of all, unlike the SGML specification that runs to over five hundred (printed) pages, the specification for XML is under thirty pages. By trimming the specifications to the bare-bones minimum, the principles and application of XML will be much more widespread than was possible with SGML. But if ease of use is a goal, hasn't HTML already become easy enough for all but the most novice user? Well, yes, HTML has become easy to use, but even with all the proprietary and often incompatible extensions, HTML is unable to handle some of the more important elements of document markup.

The ability of XML to handle industry-specific markup (through the use of specially created DTDs) allows for logically and tightly structured documents that can be employed in a number of ways. Already, a number of industries are completing work on XML DTDs for their documents. Just a few of these include

Bioinformatic Sequence Markup Language (BSML). Available at:
http://visualgenomics.com/sbir/rfc.htm.

Chemical Markup Language Version 1.0 (CML). Available at:
http://www.venus.co.uk/omf/cml/intro.html.

Mathematical Markup Language Version 1.0 (MathML). Available at:
http://www.w3.org/TR/REC-MathML.

Weather Observation Definition Format (OMF). Available at:
http://zowie.metnet.navy.mil/~spawar/JMV-TNG/XML/OMF.html.

XML for the Automotive Industry (SAE J2008). Available at:
http://www.xmlxperts.com/sae.htm.

GOOD-BYE HTML?

XML will not put HTML out of business tomorrow. With millions of copies of today's browsers likely to be on desktops well into the twenty-first century, just as SGML documents can be used to generate HTML documents (on the fly or in batch mode), the same can be done with XML documents. For that not-so-distant future when the XML user agent (aka browser) comes to dominate the desktop, it is important now to create HTML documents that are XML-compliant. When considering creating XML-compliant documents, keep the following points in mind:

XML tags, unlike HTML tags, are case sensitive; thus <ul> is a different tag (and will be rendered differently) than <UL>. Note: you can use either style, as long as you remain consistent.

XML offers much more complex linking capabilities than HTML; in addition to a linear link between two documents, XML will offer the ability to link documents in complex, bidirectional ways.

HTML documents can be easily converted into XML as long as the HTML documents are well formed (meaning, minimally, that the tags are uniform in case and that all open tags have matching closing tags).

Just as in SGML, where the author creates and declares a document type definition for each document, in XML, the header information will declare the associated XML DTD, for example, <?xml version="1.0" standalone="yes"?>.

XHTML: eXtensible HyperText Markup Language

But wait a second! Though XML is being used in a great number of situations, it is still not quite the de facto markup language for all situations. Until such time as XML takes over the markup world, we have a little something to tide us over.

XHTML, or eXtensible HyperText Markup Language, is now the official successor to HTML 4.01 for web markup languages. Growing out of the last iteration of HTML and XML, XHTML will provide a greater level of flexibility in the markup of web documents and provide a smoother transition from HTML to a full-blown XML environment.

Now for those who are used to creating HTML pages, XHTML will not be too much of a problem. But, you may be wondering, given that HTML seems to be working just fine, why do we have to change? As noted above, XML will provide a much more flexible envelope for marking up documents. And as the World Wide Web Consortium observes in XHTML 1.0: The Extensible Hyper-Text Markup Language: "Alternate ways of accessing the Internet are constantly being introduced. Some estimates indicate that by the year 2002, 75% of Internet document viewing will be carried out on these alternate platforms. The XHTML family is designed with general user agent interoperability in mind. Through a new user agent and document profiling mechanism, servers, proxies, and user agents will be able to perform best effort content transformation. Ultimately, it will be possible to develop XHTML-conforming content that is usable by any XHTML-conforming user agent."

Among the alternative platforms of the not-too-distant future are cell phones, personal digital assistants, and other Internet appliances. Though you may not envision your online exhibition being viewed from a cell phone or an Internet-enabled toaster, remember that much of the information (in the form of labels and so forth) may be of interest outside the direct context of the exhibition itself. Having a wide audience and allowing your audience to become even wider will only serve to enhance the overall effect of your exhibition.

When thinking about XHTML, XHTML 1.0: The Extensible HyperText Markup Language suggests that you keep the following key concepts in mind:

XHTML is very much like HTML.

XHTML is NOT HTML!

XHTML works with SGML concepts.

XHTML provides a transition to XML.

As an XHTML developer has noted in XHTML 1.0: The Extensible Hyper-Text Markup Language: "Document developers and user agent designers are constantly discovering new ways to express their ideas through new markup. In XML, it is relatively easy to introduce new elements or additional element attributes. The XHTML family is designed to accommodate these extensions through XHTML modules and techniques for developing new XHTML-conforming modules (described in the forthcoming XHTML Modularization specification). These modules will permit the combination of existing and new feature sets when developing content and when designing new user agents."

A few key differences between XHTML and HTML are that in XHTML

End tags must always be included.

Tags without a closing tag must be closed.

Attribute values must be in quotation marks.

All elements must be in lowercase.

Tags must be nested correctly.

Attribute name-value pairs cannot stand alone.

To make your online exhibitions as portable and long lasting as possible, it is highly recommended that you create them in XHTML!

Below are suggested readings and websites for the topics covered in this chapter.

SGML: Standard Generalized Markup Language

Bradley, Neil. 1996. *The Concise SGML Companion.* Reading, Mass.: Addison Wesley.

Getting Started with SGML. Available at: http://www.arbortext.com/data/getting_started_with_SGML/getting_started_with_sgml.html.

SGML/HTML Resource Centre. Available at: http://www.splange.freeserve.co.uk/sgml.html.

HTML: HyperText Markup Language

A Beginners Guide to HTML. Available at: http://archive.ncsa.uiuc.edu/General/Internet/WWW/HTMLPrimer.html.

Darnell, Rick, et al. 1998. *HTML 4 Unleashed.* Indianapolis: Sams.

HTML 4.01 Specification. Available at: http://www.w3.org/TR/REC-html40.

Musciano, Chuck, and Bill Kennedy. 2000. *HTML and XHTML: The Definitive Guide.* Sebastopol, Calif.: O'Reilly.

Raggett, David, ed. 1998. *Raggett on HTML 4.* Reading, Mass.: Addison Wesley.

DYNAMIC HTML

The DHTML Index. Available at: http://www.all-links.com/dynamic.

Dynamic Drive. Available at: http://www.dynamicdrive.com.

The Dynamic HTML Zone. Available at: http://www.dhtmlzone.com/index.html.

Goodman, Danny. 1998. *Dynamic HTML: The Definitive Reference.* Sebastopol, Calif.: O'Reilly.

Rule, Jeffrey S. 1999. *Dynamic HTML: The HTML Developer's Guide.* Reading, Mass.: Addison Wesley.

Teague, Jason Cranford. 2001. *DHTML and CSS for the World Wide Web: Visual QuickStart.* Berkeley, Calif.: Peachpit.

CASCADING STYLE SHEETS

Bos, Bert, Håkon Wium Lie, Chris Lilley, and Ian Jacobs, eds. 1998. "CSS2 Specification." Working draft, 28 January 1998. Available at: http://www.w3.org/TR/REC-CSS2.

Brown, Toby, Jan Roland Eriksson, Susan Lesch, and Sue Jordan. Cascading Style Sheets. Available at: http://www.css.nu/pointers.

CSSCheck. Available at: http://www.htmlhelp.com/tools/csscheck.

Falla, Bob. 1997. *HTML Style Sheets Quick Reference*. Indianapolis: Que.

HTML Writers Guild. "CSS Frequently Asked Questions." With contributions from Håkon Wium Lie and Bert Bos. Available at: http://www.w3.org/TR/REC-CSS1-961217.

Lesch, Susan. "Colors for Web Style." Available at: http://www.macvirus.com/test/color.

Lie, Håkon W. 1994. "Cascading HTML Style Sheets—A Proposal." Available at: http://www.w3.org/People/howcome/p/cascade.html.

Lie, Håkon Wium, and Bert Bos. 1999. *Cascading Style Sheets: Designing for the Web*. 2nd ed. Reading, Mass.: Addison Wesley Longman.

Meyer, Eric A. 2000. *Cascading Style Sheets: The Definitive Guide*. Sebastopol, Calif.: O'Reilly.

XML: eXtensible Markup Language

Harold, Elliotte Rusty, and W. Scott Means. 2001. *XML in a Nutshell: A Desktop Quick Reference*. Sebastopol, Calif.: O'Reilly.

Ray, T. Erik. 2001. *Learning XML*. Sebastopol, Calif.: O'Reilly.

Tittel, Ed, and Frank Boumphrey. 2000. *XML for Dummies*. Foster City, Calif.: IDG.

XML Exchange. Available at: http://www.xmlx.com.

The XML FAQ. Available at: http://www.ucc.ie/xml.

XML Version 1.0 Specification. Available at: http://www.w3.org/TR/REC-xml.html.

XHTML: eXTensible Hypertext Markup Language

Musciano, Chuck, and Bill Kennedy. 2000. *HTML and XHTML: The Definitive Guide*. Sebastopol, Calif.: O'Reilly.

Oliver, Dick, and Charles Ashbacher. 2001. *Sams Teach Yourself HTML and XHTML in 24 Hours*. Indianapolis: Sams.

Tittel, Ed, Chelsea Valentine, and Natanya Pitts. 2000. *XHTML for Dummies*. Foster City, Calif.: IDG.

XHTMLGuru. Available at: http://www.xhtmlguru.com.

XHTML 1.0: The Extensible HyperText Markup Language. Available at: http://www.w3.org/TR/xhtml1.

XHTML 1.0: Where XML and HTML Meet. Available at: http://www.webreference.com/xml/column6/index.html.

Technical Issues
Programming, Scripting, Databases, and Accessibility

In addition to the basic HTML (or other markup language) skills needed to create online exhibitions, knowledge of a number of other web design tools will be useful. Knowing how to make your online exhibition an accessible site will increase the number of potential visitors.

COMMON GATEWAY INTERFACE SCRIPTING

Making your web pages come to life with graphics, audio, and video is easier than ever. The introduction of Java and web browser plug-ins have made the Web even more multimedia. The workhorse of interactive web pages, however, is still the Common Gateway Interface (or CGI). CGI is, basically, a language or protocol that allows a web browser to transfer data to and from a web server.

Just What Is CGI?

Unlike basic HTML (or any of the markup languages that were discussed in chapter 6), which delivers preexisting files, CGI scripts are programs that act as gateways between the browser and the server. The CGI script is the middleman that interprets and repackages the information for delivery by the HTTP server back to the browser. CGI scripts give you flexibility in interacting with your audience without the nearly impossible task of altering your basic server software. A suite of CGI scripts can handle fill-out forms, guest books, visitor counters, and a range of other activities.

CGI scripts can be written in a number of programming languages (such as C, Pascal, or Basic) or in scripting languages such as TCL and Perl. Most commonly you find CGI scripts in Perl due to Perl's convenient syntax and ease of handling text. Additionally, Perl CGI scripts are widely available on the Web.

Examples and CGI Script Archives

Once you have got the hang of what you can do with a CGI script, visit some of the script archives available. A number of script wizards have created CGI scripts to share with the Internet community. Some of the more interesting sites are

Bon's CGI Freebies. Available at:
http://www.geocities.com/SiliconValley/Orchard/6104.

Matt's Script Archive. Maintained by Matt Wright. Available at: http://www.worldwidemart.com/scripts.

A Simple CGI Email Handler (2.1). Available at: http://www.boutell.com/email.

The scripts you will find on those sites will let you implement forms, counters, and guest books, display the time and date on your page, and much more. A few simple search engines are also available. Most of the scripts available at the sites are offered to the Internet community free of charge (and without warranty). Please read any restrictions or warnings before incorporating any of them into your web pages. Also, be sure to appropriately credit the creator or retain the copyright statement in the body of the script. Though Matt Wright asks on his page, "Who says you cannot get something for free anymore?" please reimburse the creators with the proper credit and even a thank-you note.

Don't Forget about Security

Unfortunately, CGI scripts can be insecure. Unsuspecting errors by the script writer or the evildoings of malicious Internet delinquents can cause damage to your server or create drains on network resources. Taking commonsense steps, such as not running your web server as root and placing all executable CGI scripts in a unique directory (e.g., cgi-bin) with stringent read/write rights, can solve most potential security breaches. For a thorough discussion of CGI security issues (and examples of dangerous scripts), see Paul Phillips's "CGI Programming MetaFAQ." An additional resource is section 6 ("CGI Scripts") of the "World Wide Web Security FAQ," maintained by Lincoln D. Stein.

JAVASCRIPT

Not up to the full-caffeine programming needed to implement Java or even the CGI scripts mentioned above? Do you still want the exciting functionality and cool design possibilities seen on cutting-edge websites? If so, pull up a stool and order some JavaScript from your local web barista. JavaScript is one of the most exciting tools for developers. Used in the right way, it can enhance the content and presentation of your site.

JavaScript versus Java

JavaScript is *not* Java. Java is a full-blown object-oriented programming language, similar to C++. Developed by Sun Microsystems, Inc., Java is particularly useful for web applications and multimedia development. To learn more about Java, visit the Java home page (http://java.sun.com). JavaScript, on the other hand, is, as its name implies, a scripting language (other scripting languages include Perl and TCL). Initially developed by Netscape Communications Corporation and Sun in late 1995, JavaScript was quickly endorsed as an open standard scripting language by all the Internet's major players.

While Java is designed for programmers, JavaScript is aimed at HTML page authors. JavaScript allows you to integrate many useful features in pages, including pop-up dialogue boxes, scrolling banners, and other simple, yet powerful ways to communicate with visitors to your pages. Additional applications, such as working with frames, forms, and (for your leisure time) games, are easily realized with JavaScript.

Integrating JavaScript in Web Pages

Unlike CGI scripts, which must reside in their own directories or be called from elsewhere on your server, JavaScripts are integrated directly into the head of each HTML page (or stored in a separate file called by the HTML file). When you use the <script language="JavaScript"> tag, browsers will recognize the intermediary text as JavaScript and execute the script as desired. The hard part, of course, is writing the script!

JavaScript Tutorials

For the JavaScript beginner one of the best resources is "Babyak's JavaScript Web Page Tutorial: Simple Little Things to Add to Your Pages." Author Michael G. Babyak modestly proclaims he is no expert and then proceeds to deliver an excellent introduction to JavaScript applications and capabilities.

As with HTML, the quickest way to get the hang of JavaScript is to look at the code of a feature that catches your eye. Use the "View Source" option on your browser to see the markup behind the feature (if the script resides on the page, of course). Unlike CGI scripts (which are often hidden from the casual browser), JavaScripts can be embedded in the text of a page's HTML markup. Look for the tag <SCRIPT language="JavaScript"> in the document to verify a JavaScript is being used. For a more structured approach to your JavaScript education, check out some of the tutorials available on the Web.

JavaScript Archives and Other Resources

For many of the most basic JavaScript applications (including the ubiquitous scrolling banner and its countless variations), script archives or downloadable sites exist. Among the more useful JavaScript sites are the following, many of which include links to a plethora of JavaScript resources:

JavaScript Code Ripper. Available at:
    http://www.twics.com/~renfield/java/jsmain.html.

The JavaScript Planet. Available at:
    http://www.geocities.com/SiliconValley/7116.

Timothy's JavaScript Examples. Available at:
    http://www.essex1.com/people/timothy/js-index.htm.

For the more seasoned JavaScript developer, there is this more advanced site:

JavaScript Tip of the Week. Available at:
    http://webreference.com/javascript.

Be Careful!

Though, generally speaking, JavaScripts do not pose a hazard to your server, there have been some concerns about their security. As with any client/server application, be aware of the risks of mounting interactive applications on your server. Information about JavaScript security can be found in the JavaScript FAQ. Also, please test your JavaScript applications with a couple of browsers before turning them loose on the world. JavaScript applications are dynamic tools, but they are sometimes unstable. Don't undermine the content of your page with an erratic JavaScript.

DATABASES FOR ONLINE EXHIBITIONS

You've just created a perfect exhibition. It contains over a hundred objects and is divided into a number of different sections. You want to give viewers both a master list of all the objects, categorized by author, and sublists of the objects in each section, also categorized by author. You will need to have a lot of spare time on your hands, because manually compiling those lists will take you a long, long time! There must be a better way. And there is.

Why a Database?

Creating a database for your online exhibition can save you a great deal of time in the long run. Generating an underlying database for your exhibition would also enable you to

Track objects as you plan the exhibition

Repurpose the data for other uses

Write once, output many times

As Breiteneder, Platzer, and Hitz (2001) note, the use of a database in exhibition design "shifts development work to a higher level of abstraction: instead of 'coding' Web pages in HTML, the main tasks consist of editing and structuring content liberated from layout questions."

Track Objects as You Plan the Exhibition.   If a database is used early in the exhibition planning process, the curator can add and delete objects very easily. The information gathered at the time the exhibition is being planned will be useful for a number of tracking purposes throughout the life span of the exhibition.

Repurpose the Data for Other Uses.   You might be surprised at how often you will need the same information about objects. A database of objects used in exhibitions can be repurposed for a number of other uses.

Write Once, Output Many Times.   You know the old adage "Measure twice, cut once." The same holds true for data entry. Once your object information is available in a database, you can output it in various formats (or even reformat entire portions of the exhibition) without writing pages and pages of markup.

Database Design for Online Exhibitions

As with most topics related to database design, the key to a good database is understanding the uses (and imagining the potential uses) of the data that you collect. Take a careful look at the type of object you will be using in your exhibition. Are you displaying books, serials, manuscripts, realia? Perhaps you will have a more unusual type of material, such as photographs or sheet music.

Though it is nearly impossible to design a database that will take into account every possibility, thorough planning ahead of time will cover many eventualities. A well-designed database could also be used for multiple exhibitions to allow for easy searching or collocating of objects either for general viewers of your online exhibitions or for behind-the-scenes work in exhibition development.

For a list of suggested fields in an exhibition database, see appendix D.

Web/Database Interfaces

There are a number of options for users who wish to create web/database interfaces. At the simplest level, it is possible to use the "Generate HTML" function of Microsoft Access to create functional (yet limited) static web pages based on data in your database.

For more sophisticated applications, however, you will want to move to a larger scale, web/database interface product. The primary options currently available are (in alphabetical order) Active Server Pages (ASP, from Microsoft), Cold Fusion (Allaire), Filemaker Pro, and PHP.

Each of these products allows you to utilize a database management tool (such as Microsoft Access) and then, through a combination of HTML and other coding, connect to the data in the database to generate on-the-fly web pages.

ACCESSIBILITY ISSUES

The Web is inherently visual and multimedia. Flashy images, vibrant colors, and fancy fonts are more the rule than the exception for websites that capture the most coveted of cyberspace adjectives, *cool*. However, as noted in the August 1996 issue of *Netscape World,* "There are 40 million people with disabilities in the U.S., and many of them have problems that keep them from using a carelessly designed Web page. This isn't because the techniques to make pages accessible to the disabled are not available, but rather it's because Web designers don't think of the problems that they may be creating." If the Web is to reach the promise of its hype, the needs of this large segment of the population cannot be ignored. It is also important to note that *accessibility* is not a code word for dull. As with any design problem, the best solution can also be the most aesthetically pleasing.

For people who are blind or have low vision, surfing the Web can involve a number of technologies, including the use of a synthetic speech synthesizer or a refreshable Braille display that reads the ASCII text on the screen. Providing text for images and bit-mapped text is an important key to creating accessible pages. Future implementations of XML and style sheets will enable a host of different user agents to bring web pages to these audiences. In the meantime, however, there are a number of techniques that can be used to make your pages accessible.

Something as simple as text and hypertext link colors can become an accessibility issue when color blindness is taken into consideration. The use of style sheets on your web pages can increase their accessibility level by allowing users to globally override your style with one that better suits their needs. With some forms of color blindness, text and links can fade to invisibility. For a further discussion of this issue and solutions to this problem, see Samu Mielonen's "Colour Blindness and Link Colours" for some hints on how to make link colors (as well as text and backgrounds) more accessible. The Color Vision Simulator, an online checker from Vischeck, will display your image in different formats that will help you see how they may look to people with differing forms of color blindness.

Also remember that though the obvious concern with web pages is for people who are blind or have low vision, the increased use of sound clips on websites necessitates allowances for Net surfers who are deaf or hard of hearing. Be sure to add textual transcriptions for audio clips and descriptions of sound effects. This is particularly important when sound clips are an important part of the online exhibition experience.

Some simple and general principles to keep in mind when designing your exhibition pages include

Use the ALT tag for images to provide text descriptions.

Provide text links for image maps and button/image links.

Make text links meaningful. For example, avoid the use of "Click Here."

Guides to Writing Accessible Web Documents

A number of guides are available to assist with the creation of accessible web pages. Among the the most useful primers are

> Designing More Usable Web Sites
>
> "Design of Accessible Web Pages," by Jane Berliss et al. (National Institute on Disability and Rehabilitation Research)
>
> "Guide to Accessible HTML: HyperText Mark-Up Language," by Jan Richards
>
> Web Content Accessibility Guidelines 1.0
>
> "Writing Accessible HTML Documents," by Paul Fontaine (U.S. General Services Administration)

Accessible Band-Aids for the Bleeding Edge

The latest web technologies, such as Java and VRML (Virtual Reality Modeling Language), pose unique challenges to the creator of accessible web pages. For Java and JavaScript, the Java Accessibility Project is a useful resource. For VRML, see "Accessibility and VRML," from the Adaptive Technology Resource Centre (ATRC). The Adobe Acrobat PDF (Portable Document Format) file format is also a source of concern; some solutions are outlined in the "Adobe Acrobat Access White Paper: PDF and the Visually Disabled." The ACT Centre is a good resource for accessibility solutions to advanced HTML features, including columns, tables, forms, and frames. Issues concerning audio and video clips are also covered at that site.

Americans with Disabilities Act (ADA)

The Americans with Disabilities Act (ADA) of 1990 includes requirements that U.S. federal, state, and local governments meet accessibility standards when providing information. The full text of the law is available at http://www.usdoj.gov/crt/ada/statute.html. Links to related legislation and policy documents are available from the U.S. General Services Administration at http://www.dinf.org/gsa/coca/law_pol.htm. To help interpret ADA requirements, the U.S. Department of Justice maintains the "Americans with Disabilities Act Home Page" (http://www.usdoj.gov/crt/ada/adahom1.htm).

Are My Pages Accessible?

In addition to following the suggestions of the resources above, you can use Bobby, a handy online tool, to verify that your web pages are accessible. Created by Josh Krieger for the Center for Applied Special Technology (CAST), Bobby will analyze your web pages and notify you of any code that may cause difficulties for some users.

Although you may be tempted to use cutting-edge web design for your online exhibition, you need to remember that a site that cannot be viewed by all will lose many potential viewers.

Below are suggested readings and websites for the topics covered in this chapter.

COMMON GATEWAY INTERFACE (CGI)

Bon's CGI Freebies. Available at:
> http://www.geocities.com/SiliconValley/Orchard/6104.

Matt's Script Archive. Available at: http://www.worldwidemart.com/scripts.

Phillips, Paul. CGI Programming MetaFAQ. Available at: http://www.smithrenaud.com/public/CGI_MetaFAQ.html.

A Simple CGI Email Handler (2.1). Available at: http://www.boutell.com/email.

Stein, Lincoln D. "World Wide Web Security FAQ." Available at: http://www-genome.wi.mit.edu/WWW/faqs/wwwsf4.html.

JAVASCRIPT

Babyak, Michael G. "Babyak's JavaScript Web Page Tutorial: Simple Little Things to Add to Your Pages."Available at: http://ftn.kaist.ac.kr/~cgeeju/HTML/JAVASCRIPT/java.html.

Flanagan, David. 1998. *Javascript: The Definitive Guide*. Sebastopol, Calif.: O'Reilly.

Goodman, Danny, and Brendan Eich. 2001. *Javascript Bible*. New York: Hungry Minds.

JavaScript Code Ripper. Available at: http://www.twics.com/~renfield/java/jsmain.html.

The JavaScript FAQ. Available at: http://developer.netscape.com/support/faqs/champions/javascript.html.

The JavaScript Planet. Available at: http://wwwgeocities.com/SiliconValley/7116.

Timothy's JavaScript Examples. Available at: http://www.essex1.com/people/timothy/js-index.htm.

JavaScript Tip of the Week. Available at: http://webreference.com/javascript.

Winsor, Janice, and Brian Freeman. 1997. *Jumping JavaScript*. Mountain View, Calif.: Sun Microsystems Press.

DATABASES

Breiteneder, Christian, Hubert Platzer, and Martin Hitz. 2001. "A Re-Usable Software Framework for Authoring and Managing Web Exhibitions." Museums and the Web. Available at: http://www.archimuse.com/mw2001/papers/breiteneder/breiteneder2.html.

ACTIVE SERVER PAGES (ASP)

ASP from A to Z. Available at: http://msdn.microsoft.com/workshop/server/asp/aspatoz.asp.

Buser, David, John Kauffman, Juan T. Llibre, Brian Francis, David Sussman, Chris Ullman, and Jon Duckett. 2000. *Beginning Active Server Pages 3.0*. Birmingham, U.K.: Wrox.

Mitchell, Scott, and James Atkinson. 2000. *Sams Teach Yourself Active Server Pages 3.0 in 21 Days*. Indianapolis: Sams.

COLD FUSION

Allaire (Cold Fusion). Available at: http://www.allaire.com.

Forta, Ben, Nate Weiss, and David E. Crawford. 2001. *The Coldfusion 4.0 Web Application Construction Kit (Cold Fusion 4)*. Indianapolis: Que.

Forta, Ben, Nate Weiss, and Gerry Libertelli. 1999. *Advanced Cold Fusion 4 Application Development*. Indianapolis: Que.

FILEMAKER PRO

Coulombre, Rich, and Jonathan Price. 2000. *Special Edition: Using Filemaker Pro 5*. Indianapolis: Que.

FileMaker Pro. Available at: http://www.filemaker.com.

Stars, Jonathan. 2001. *Learn Filemaker Pro 5.0*. Plano, Tex.: Wordware.

PHP

Lea, Chris, et al. 2000. *Beginning PHP4*. Birmingham, U.K.: Wrox.

PHPDeveloper.org. Available at: http://www.phpdeveloper.org.

PHP FAQ. Available at: http://www.php.net/FAQ.php.

PHP Resource Index. Available at: http://php.resourceindex.com.

Welling, Luke, and Laura Thomson. 2001. *PHP and MySQL Web Development*. Indianapolis: Sams.

ACCESSIBILITY ISSUES

Adaptive Technology Resource Centre (ATRC). "Accessibility and VRML." Available at: http://www.utoronto.ca/atrc/rd/vrml/main.html.

Adaptive Technology Resource Centre (ATRC). University of Toronto. Available at: http://www.utoronto.ca/atrc.

Adobe Acrobat Accessibility. Available at: http://www.adobe.com:80/products/acrobat/solutionsacc.html.

Berliss, Jane, Lewis Kraus, and Susan Stoddard. "Design of Accessible Web Pages." National Institute on Disability and Rehabilitation Research. Available at: http://www.infouse. com/disabilitydata/addaccess.html.

Bobby. Available at: http://www.cast.org/bobby.

ColorMax—Colorblind Science. Available at: http://www.colormaxtech.com/colorblindscience/colorblind.htm.

Color Vision Simulator. Available at: http://vischeck.com/showme.shtml.

Colour Blind Design Hints and Tips. Available at: http://www.cimmerii.demon.co.uk/colourblind/design.html.

Designing for the Color-Challenged: A Challenge. Available at: http://www.InternetTG.org/newsletter/mar99/accessibility_color_challenged.html.

Designing More Usable Web Sites. Available at: http://trace.wisc.edu/world/web.

Equal Access to Software and Information (EASI). Available at: http://www.rit.edu/~easi/index.html.

Fontaine, Paul. "Writing Accessible HTML Documents." U.S. General Services Administration. Available at: http://www.webable.com/library/htmlcode.html.

Java Accessibility Project. Available at: http://trace.wisc.edu/world/java/java.htm.

Mielonen, Samu. "Colour Blindness and Link Colours." Available at: http://www.washington.edu/doit/Resources/color.blind.html.

National Library Service for the Blind and Physically Handicapped. Library of Congress. Available at: http://lcweb.loc.gov/nls/nls.html.

Richards, Jan. "Guide to Accessible HTML: HyperText Mark-Up Language." Available at: http://www.utoronto.ca/atrc/rd/html/html.html.

Rigden, Christine. "Safe Web Colours for Colour-Deficient Vision." Available at: http://innovate.bt.com/people/rigdence/colours.

Vischeck. Available at: http://www.vischeck.com/vischeckURL.php3.

Web Content Accessibility Guidelines 1.0. Available at: http://www.w3.org/TR/WAI-WEBCONTENT.

CHAPTER 8

Design

No pains must be spared in the presentation of material in the exhibition halls. The specimens must be prepared in the most careful and artistic manner, and arranged attractively in well-designed cases and behind the clearest of glass. Each object must bear a label, giving its name and history so fully that all the probable questions of the visitor are answered in advance. Books of reference must be kept in convenient places. Colors of walls, cases, and labels must be restful and quiet, and comfortable seats should be everywhere accessible, for the task of the museum visitor is a weary one at best.—George Brown Goode

Though the visitors to your online exhibition will not need comfortable seats, nearly all of the points made by Goode in the above quotation are applicable to online as well as gallery exhibitions. Though you may have come up with a brilliant idea for your exhibition, though you may have written the most intelligent and entertaining script ever and assembled the best objects, if you are unable to translate all of those things into a design that works in an online environment, your visitors will be lost, or worse, will choose to go elsewhere.

RETROSPECTIVE CONVERSION OF GALLERY EXHIBITIONS

In many instances, your library or archive will have been creating gallery exhibitions for a number of years. Much of the material from those exhibitions (as well as the curators themselves) may still be around. In such instances, it is a matter of adapting the material to the online environment and digitizing the appropriate images. Though the latter may be simple enough, adapting material is not always as simple as it may appear. The National Gallery of Canada acknowledges the problem of adapting material from the printed medium to the interactive (Pierroux): "It is difficult to use existing documentation for a real visitor and adapt it to a cyberspace environment. Ideally, content would be created specifically and solely for the Web visitor, but time and resources are not always available for this type of approach."

A similar problem occurs when attempting to simultaneously create a gallery exhibition and an online exhibition. In many cases, the attempt to bring about online and gallery exhibitions at the same time will involve quite a bit of work and pulling of hair.

HOW ONLINE AND GALLERY EXHIBITIONS DIFFER

Before we jump into some principles and practices for designing online exhibitions, let's reiterate a few points that may seem obvious but bear repeating.

First, a computer monitor (or TV screen) is not an exhibition gallery. A monitor does not have physical and visual elements (such as Goode's comfortable seats) to immediately draw a visitor into an experience. The web experience is an interesting blend of the passive and the interactive. Simply by walking into an exhibition gallery, visitors are able to absorb (consciously or subconsciously) much of the content as well as the basic layout of at least the first room of the exhibition. Sitting or standing, a visitor can scan the room and on some level grasp its entire contents. Likewise, when visitors click into your online exhibition, they are thrust into a similar environment where they can absorb the information before them. Unlike the gallery visitor, however, the visitor to the online exhibition must move from passive absorption of the exhibition to active participation through clicking or scrolling. Though a gallery exhibition may lose visitors if they turn and walk out, the online exhibition can lose visitors through the simple click of a mouse.

Second, remember that your tools are limited. The designer of a gallery exhibition can be fairly certain that the vast majority of visitors will experience the physical elements of an exhibition (colors, fonts used in labels, case layout) in roughly the same manner. In the online environment, that assumption can't be made. Until everyone in the entire world has the same kind of computer, the same settings on that computer, the same bandwidth on their Internet connection, and the same web browser, the experiences of the visitors to your online exhibition will vary, sometimes even drastically. When designing an online exhibition, you will have to keep a number of possible experiences in mind.

And third, nobody likes to get lost. In a gallery exhibition, visitors will get lost only in the most labyrinthine layout and will always have security staff, docents, or other visitors to help them find their way through (or out of) the exhibition. In the online world, once visitors have lost the thread of navigation through your exhibition, the quickest and most satisfying remedy is a click that sends them out of your exhibition and into something easier to navigate.

So, with those thoughts in mind, let's explore web design for online exhibitions.

THE DESIGN PROCESS

One of the key components of design in general, and of good design in particular, is the solution to a set of known (and unknown) problems. In an exhibition, the design will manifest itself not only in the solution of problems, such as those related to display and visibility, but also in the communication of an idea.

The design process itself is highly individualistic, and different designers will use different methods to achieve their goals. Still, a number of typical steps or processes can be enumerated. Bruce Archer (1965), in *Systematic Method for*

Designers, listed 229(!) events in a design process. For practical purposes, we can distill those down to the following:

Problem Analysis.   What is the purpose of this exhibition and how will it be presented?

Synthesis.   After analyzing the problem, put together all the pieces and see what you get.

Development.   Start putting your ideas on the screen. Experiment with colors and designs, and don't forget to save your ideas as you go along. What seemed stupid and awful on a late Friday night might be the very thing you want when you look at it with a fresh eye Monday morning.

Revision.   Revise again and again and again. There is a reason behind the saying *Ars longa vita brevis* (Art is long, life is short). Revision will allow you to hone a design to make it the best it can be.

Finalization.   Remember you don't have forever. Deadlines and the human need to have a project come to a close will force you to pick one design over another. Come to a conclusion on a design and then implement it throughout the online exhibition.

Also remember that in the design process, the difference between a small job and a big job can be deceptive. In many cases, it is a small exhibition that is more difficult to design than a large exhibition. With fewer objects to choose from, less text, and so forth, each element of the exhibition is more on display and will receive more attention than it would in a sprawling exhibition of hundreds of objects. Though in all exhibitions (large and small), each object should be carefully thought of in the design process, in a small exhibition, the design process and its results will be more on display.

With online exhibitions, in addition to the usual problems of design, a number of limitations are imposed by the media on the designer. Making the most of the additional opportunities afforded the web designer and minimizing the limitations will make for the best online exhibition.

Let's examine some of the opportunities and limitations to be found in online exhibition design.

Screen Layout

Do you hate to scroll? Most people don't mind scrolling vertically. Vertical scrolling is a fairly acceptable mode of moving around information on a computer screen. Horizontal scrolling, however, is another story. Unless the information on the screen is laid out so that horizontal scrolling is the navigation method, nothing will be more irksome to visitors than having to scroll *both* horizontally and vertically to view your site.

So, why are your visitors having horizontal scrolling issues? Two words: monitor resolution. Screen resolution is one of the key environmental factors that determine how information appears on the screen. Most of us who know our way around the different settings on our computers know that all screens are not created equally and, more importantly, know that many screen settings can be adjusted. Many users, however, are unaware of monitor settings and how to adjust them, and live with whatever the factory defaults are.

Monitor resolution refers to the number of pixels that appear on the vertical and horizontal axes of the screen. For many years, screen size for most computers was fixed at 640 pixels wide by 480 pixels high. Resolution is a factor of hardware (monitor, CPU, and video/graphics card) and can be adjusted within the bounds of the hardware. Many high-end computers still ship, however, with monitor resolution set at the lowest common denominator of 640 × 480 pixels even though the monitor and video/graphics card itself may be capable of resolutions in the 1,280 × 1,024 category or higher.

When designing online exhibitions, it's important to think about screen resolution or your visitors will end up with unpleasant horizontal scrolling. Another element of screen resolution to keep in mind is the size of your images. An image that is 400 pixels wide will take up approximately two-thirds of a screen set to 640 × 480 resolution. That same 400-pixel-wide image on a 1,280 × 1,024 screen will take up only about a third of the screen. On the lower-resolution screen, the image will appear large, and on the higher-resolution screen, small. If your design depends on a banner logo or title image to take up the entire width of the screen, remember that if the image is, say, 700 pixels wide, it will appear perfect on an 800 × 600 resolution monitor; slightly smaller on a 1,280 × 1,024 monitor; and force the viewer to scroll on a 640 × 480 monitor.

Another culprit in screen design that can raise havoc with different monitor resolutions is tables. Many web designers use the <table width="x"> element to provide left and right margins or white space on their screens. If, however, the width of the table is cited in pixels (e.g., <table width="775">), a web browser on a lower-resolution screen will extend this table beyond the width of the viewing area and force the user to scroll horizontally. Citing the table width in percentages (e.g., <table width="90%">) will give you better results on a variety of monitor resolutions, but may not solve all scrolling problems. A better solution for providing a tablelike layout is to use style sheets (see chapter 6).

Tiling graphics (e.g., graphics used as backgrounds to a page or to parts of a table) will often appear in strange configurations on monitor resolutions for which they were not designed.

Lastly, web browsers themselves take up a certain percentage of the screen. Though this is most obvious on the top portion of the screen (where the toolbars and so forth reside), there is also a small, yet significant portion of the screen on each side taken up by the web browser border and scroll bar. See figures 14, 15, and 16 for examples of the same exhibition page seen in different web browsers.

For assistance in screen resolution design issues, visit the Browsergrid from the Web Page Design for Designers page (Gillespie 2000).

Color

A very similar problem to that of screen resolution is color display on monitors. How many colors are there in the world? How many colors can a monitor display? How many colors can your web browser display safely without distortion? Is the color that I see on my PC screen the same color that you see on your Mac screen?

Unfortunately, all the questions posed above have no satisfactory answers (except for the first one, whose answer is *infinite*, which in most cases is not really a satisfactory answer).

As with monitor resolution, color display is dependent on the video/graphics card, the monitor, and the CPU. On a typical PC, you will find a number of

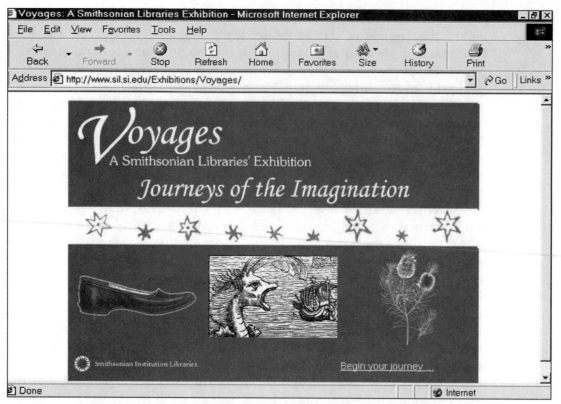

FIGURE 14 | Screen shot, Internet Explorer (version 5.0). *Voyages: A Smithsonian Libraries Exhibition.* Courtesy Smithsonian Institution Libraries.

FIGURE 15 | Screen shot, Internet Explorer (version 5.0), full-screen mode. *Voyages: A Smithsonian Libraries Exhibition.* Courtesy Smithsonian Institution Libraries.

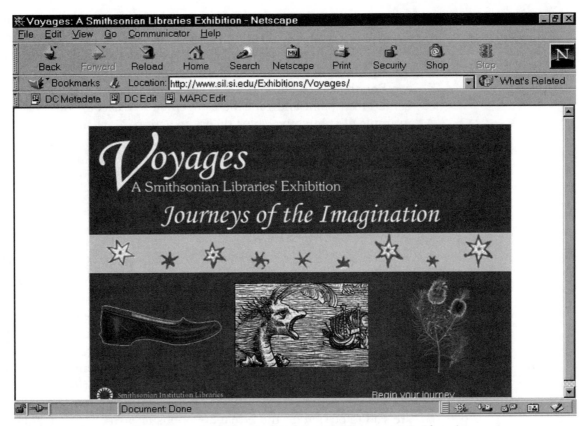

FIGURE 16 | Screen shot, Netscape Navigator (version 4.7). *Voyages: A Smithsonian Libraries Exhibition.* Courtesy Smithsonian Institution Libraries.

options for the display of color. In the past, most color monitors could display only 256 (8-bit) colors (this is, for you old-timers out there, after the age of the amber-on-black monitors). Most monitors now have color options ranging from the low-end 256 colors to 65,536 (16-bit) colors, 16,777,216 (24-bit) colors, and "true color." Similar to the case of monitor resolution, some computers will ship with the low end of color display and their users will never take advantage of all their color possibilities. The problems of printing in accurate color from the typical desktop computer to the typical desktop laser or inkjet printer are even more complex.

What do these color facts mean to you, the online exhibition designer? First and foremost, it means that the colors you are seeing on your screen (in your office with your ambient light) will not be the same colors seen by anyone else in the world. This is not to say that they won't be close in many cases, but it is important to remember that color, one of the most important design elements, is much more fluid in online design than in gallery exhibitions.

A LITTLE BIT OF COLOR THEORY

In the real world, color is subtractive. As objects absorb light, they reflect back the color with some of the color subtracted. Starting with the primary colors (red, blue, and yellow) and mixing them in varying amounts results in a spectrum of colors.

A computer screen, however, can't absorb light, but rather generates light. Computers (and TVs, for that matter) use what is called additive synthesis to display color. In additive synthesis, the colors red, green, and blue (popularly referred to as RGB) are mixed together to form a spectrum of colors.

For those of you with an experimental nature, take some red paint and some green paint and mix them together. What color do you get? This is an example of subtractive color theory in action. Now, mix red and green using a computer graphics program. What color do you get? This is additive synthesis in action. (For the less-than-curious or those without access to poster paints and graphics programs, mixing red paint and green paint makes brown, and mixing red pixels and green pixels makes yellow.)

COLOR ELEMENTS

Color is very complex, and years of design training and a natural talent are needed to master all its elements. A few things to keep in mind (which you may remember from the color unit in elementary school) are the three types of color: *primary* (red, blue, and yellow), *secondary* (mixtures of equal portions of primary colors—red + yellow = orange, blue + yellow = green, red + blue = purple), and *tertiary* (gradations of color that are created when unequal portions for primary colors are mixed). Note: these examples are from the subtractive world of real color, not from the additive world of computer color.

On a color wheel, colors that are next to each other (e.g., blue and purple) are said to be *similar*; those that are opposite each other (e.g., orange and blue) are termed *complementary*; and those separated by three colors (e.g., red and green) are *contrasting*.

By adding white to any primary or secondary color, you create a different *tint*; by adding black, you create a different *shade*.

Three additional factors, *hue, value,* and *saturation,* determine, respectively, the color differentiation, darkness, and intensity.

By mixing all these elements of color, a designer can evoke a range of feelings and emotions. Bright red and bright yellow can remind us of hotdog stands. Cool blues and greens, of woodsy forests. Colors can also evoke different meanings for members of different cultures. For a quick discussion of how color can mean different things in different cultures, see Molly E. Holzschlag's "Color My World" in "Other Websites Discussed." Additional information on the meaning of color can be found at the website Color Matters.

One last element to be concerned with is the *gamma* value of monitors. Gamma valuations of color and monitors is a complex topic that is in many cases subjective. For our purposes, gamma can be thought of as the relative brightness of the image on the screen. Or, it might be easiest to repeat the mantra "Macintoshes have better gamma correction than PCs do." For an in-depth discussion of issues relating to gamma, see "Why Do Images Appear Darker on Some Displays? An Explanation of Monitor Gamma," by Robert W. Berger.

NAMING COLORS

If you've ever ordered anything from a mail-order catalog, you've probably scratched your head at some of the color options. I want a red sweater, but the only choices that sound close are burnt clay and frosted burgundy. Which one is red? Computers are less tolerant of ambiguity than even the most fastidious of us humans. For a computer, a color has to have a very specific meaning and value.

As noted above, computers view colors in an additive synthesis of red, green, and blue (RGB). Thus, for computers, all color values can be expressed in terms of 256 potential values for red and green and blue. Black expressed in RGB values is 000, 000, 000. White is expressed as 255, 255, 255 of the three colors. Red is expressed as 255, 000, 000. By varying the proportions of each of the three colors, a wide variety of colors can be created. To make life more complex for web designers in the early days of HTML, color for such elements as backgrounds and fonts had to be displayed in hexadecimal format rather than in RGB values.

Hexadecimal is a base-16 number system that consists of sixteen unique symbols: the numbers 0 to 9 and the letters A to F. In hexadecimal notation, black (000, 000, 000 in RGB) is 00, 00, 00; white is FF, FF, FF; and red is FF, 00, 00.

In an attempt to make color notation easier for web designers, the powers that be (Microsoft, the W3C, and Netscape) formulated standard names that web browsers would render. Thus, aqua was defined as 000, 000, 255 (00, FF, FF hexadecimal) and teal as 000, 000, 128 (00, 80, 80 hexadecimal). Color names were later expanded to a list of 136. See the Netscape Color Names site for the complete list. On that list, we find lavenderblush (255, 240, 245 in RGB, and FF, F0, F5 hexadecimal). Needless to say, as a web designer, your life will be simpler if you focus on the unambiguous numeric color values.

BROWSER-SAFE COLOR PALETTE

When we were kids, our world of colors was determined by the size of our crayon box. Some kids got just the basic 8-pack of colors, some got the box of 16, some got the big box of 64, and the really lucky kids got the box of 128 crayons with a built-in sharpener.

Now we've grown up to design online exhibitions, and we have not 8, 16, 64, or even 128 colors to play with, but millions! The world's our oyster and we can thumb our noses at the limitations imposed by Crayola!

Alas, as noted above, the different monitors, operating platforms, and browsers impose on our creative potential as much as any crayon maker. So what are we to do? We'll just take a chance. Throw caution to the wind and design our exhibition with a mistyrose (FF, E4, E1 hexadecimal) background and darkseagreen (8F, BC, 8F) text and let the pixels fall where they may.

Well, that might be one option, but another would be to use the browser-safe color palette and save ourselves some trouble in the world of color.

The browser-safe color palette was devised by Lynda Weinman to include the colors that would safely (e.g., correctly) display on a variety of computers with different web browsers. The browser-safe color palette is composed of 216 colors. Those colors represent the 256 colors available on an 8-bit computer system. Forty colors are reserved for the operating system and the browser, leaving 216 colors that will render true on any system.

The browser-safe color palette is useful when creating images with large swaths of a single color (for instance, in logos), when specifying background colors or font colors, and in other instances when you can control the color of an object. If you use a color that is not among the 216 in the browser-safe color palette, when that color is rendered on the screen, the computer will dither it (that is, choose the next closest color according to its own set of parameters). Depending on the system, browser, and so forth, the color may dither to something you would neither expect nor want. In an image (say, a photograph), the dithering will not be noticeable because you are unlikely to have large numbers of similar color pixels next to each other. If, however, you use a large swatch of a nonsafe color as a background, the dithering will be obvious.

Screen size, color, . . . what else is going to cause the online exhibition designer problems?

Fonts and Typography

Yes, fonts. Fonts, or the look of the actual letters used for your text, are a major problem with web design. Before we get into the problems that you will have with fonts as you design your online exhibition, let's clarify a few terms.

FONT VERSUS TYPEFACE

In common parlance, *font* and *typeface* (or *type*) are often used interchangeably. To professional designers, however, there is a very specific meaning attached to each of these terms. A font is design for a set of characters. A typeface includes both the font design and a number of other qualities that pertain to it (such as size, pitch, spacing, and weighting). Thus Times Roman is a description for a certain kind of character's shape. The Times Roman typeface will include a number of sizes (5 point, 10 point, 12 point, and so on); different styles, such as italic; different weights, such as bold; and other characteristics.

Another term, *typography,* refers to the technical production, or process, of printing from type, or to the general appearance, arrangement, or style of words or characters on a page. In the world of the Web, any preconceived notions about typography need to be thrown out. Still, it is necessary to consider some of the principles of typography (e.g., proper use of headings to reflect relations among topics, use of white space around text, and use of boldface and italics). Web pages differ from printed pages in a number of ways. Some of these differences are outlined in "Typography on the Web," by Frank Boumphrey. For example:

The shape of the page is different; it is usually a landscape (i.e., horizontal) configuration rather than a portrait (i.e., vertical) configuration.

The resolution of the medium is lower. Finely detailed fonts do not therefore render well.

Because of the above, reading speed is about 30 percent slower than for the printed page.

Readers tend to scan rather than read.

The retention rate is about 50 percent lower than for the printed page.

Scroll bars add a new factor.

FONTS ON THE WEB

If you look at the default settings of your web browser, you will generally find two kinds of fonts listed, fixed-pitch fonts and proportional fonts. Generally, the default fixed-pitch font will be Courier and the default proportional font Times Roman. One of the first things to remember about fonts in web design is that unless you specify a font in your page markup, the default font on the viewer's web browser will be used.

But what if you want to use a font that is not Times Roman? Your computer has a really nifty font (say, Matisse or Bees Knees) that you've set as your default because you like to view the world that way. How can you code your exhibition so that everybody sees your pages through your worldview? The simple answer is that you can't.

Current web technology demands that only fonts available on an individual's machine are available for display (we'll get into downloadable or dynamic fonts in a bit). That means that unless the entire world (or at least the portion of it that is viewing your web pages) has the font you specify in your design on their machine, the text will render not as your selected font, but as the user's default font.

The other great font-related variable in web design is font size. In the print world, the size of a character is measured in points, with each point being around $1/72$ of an inch. Needless to say, this measurement is not quite adequate on a computer screen for a number of reasons. The first issue that faces us is screen resolution (see above). But even if we get around that, just as users have the ability to set a default font, they can also select a size to display their text. In Internet Explorer, there are five options ranging from "smallest" to "largest"; Netscape (version 4.x) allows users to set the default size in points and enables them to increase or decrease the text size by using the control plus square brackets key combination.

Given the limitations affecting font selection and font size, what can you do when selecting the best fonts for use in your online exhibitions?

USING FONTS

The first and best recommendation that can be made regarding the whole font issue in web design is to use style sheets. Let me repeat that. *Use style sheets* to handle your font styles and sizes. Though it is true that older browsers will not be able to handle style sheets, a good design can be created that will degrade well enough to be viewable in a user's default font. See chapter 6 for more details on using style sheets.

OK, you've agreed to use style sheets for handling your text display. What other issues should you keep in mind?

First off, there are three major categories of fonts: *serif, sans serif,* and *display* (sometimes known as *decorative*). Serif fonts are those that have little finishing strokes or fillips going off the ending lines of a letter. Times Roman, Basset, and Charter are examples of fonts with serifs. Sans serif fonts, which first appeared around 1815 to 1817, lack serifs. The character forms are simpler and often have an underlying geometric design. Examples of sans serif fonts include Arial, Futura, and Helvetica.

Spencer and Reynolds (1977, 100) note that "many readers claim that they find sans serif faces subjectively less legible than serifed faces, but objective measures of reading performance are often conflicting and it cannot be said that one type style is significantly more or less legible than the other."

As a general rule, sans serif fonts are good choices for titles and other major headings, and serifed fonts for large blocks of text. However, for accessibility purposes, sans serif fonts are generally recommended.

Display or decorative fonts are a little harder to describe. You might say that they are the fonts that annoy you when someone uses them for extensive blocks of text. Such fonts are most suitable for titles and other headings. Examples of display fonts are **Lisbon**, Tempo, and **BlippoBlack.** Remember that display fonts are less likely to be on all your viewers' computers, so they should be avoided for most web work. Also, try not to mix too many kinds of fonts on a page (or even a website). Remember, you do not want your page to look like a ransom note!

Boldface and *italics* should be used sparingly and appropriately. Use boldface when you want to call attention to a word or phrase. Italics should be used sparingly in web design because they are often difficult to read on-screen. As most of the items in your online exhibitions will be books (or other items in which titles or other elements are commonly italicized), you may wish to use another typographic element to denote titles if italics will cause problems with your screen display. Please do not use underlining on a web page except as a final resort. Users are accustomed to hypertext links being underlined, and many will be annoyed if underlined text is not a hyperlink.

Lastly, remember that in the online world, color is cheap, so you can be more creative and liberal in the use of color for your text. At the same time, keep in mind that large swaths of bright yellow text will be illegible for most viewers.

FONTS AND STYLE SHEETS

Many of the basic principles in the style sheet technical specification are related directly to control of fonts. With style sheets, you can control the font type, size, color, and weight; line spacing; character spacing; indents; margins; and so forth. Advanced use of style sheets can also allow you to layer text to achieve a drop shadow effect or other design effects that were previously available only with text images. Explore style sheets to see how much you can accomplish before resorting to the text image method.

DOWNLOADABLE, EMBEDDED, OR DYNAMIC FONTS (AS PROMISED EARLIER)

The ability to embed a font in a page design practically eliminates the necessity of using text images. A number of standards and proprietary plans are in the works to allow web designers to use fonts so that their viewers will see exactly what was designed, but, as of this writing, we are not there yet.

Labels and Text Design

In chapter 4, we discussed labels and their content. The design of labels and how they will appear on the screen can be almost as important as the content. Remember, if people are not lured into reading the text by its appearance, they may not read it at all. Daniel Jacobi and Marie Sylvie Poli (1995, 51), in their article "Scriptovisual Documents in Exhibitions: Some Theoretical Guidelines," note that "the text, while meant to be read, is also characterized by its spatiovisual organization in the space that it occupies. Thus, an exhibition text is also made to be seen. Texts displayed in museums differ from the texts or printed material we usually read. Reading/seeing, seeing/reading: in a museum, these two cognitive activities are permanently intertwined."

In the online environment that statement is even more true! When thinking of your labels (as well as the other text in your online exhibition), remember that the text and how it appears are as important as the images you select. Label text should be designed to complement the content of the label. Through the use of fonts, colors, sizes, and emphasis (boldface and italics), the relative importance of the various elements of the label will be communicated to the viewer/reader.

Studies and common sense show that, in the online environment, people will not read large blocks of text (a truism sadly evident in gallery exhibitions also). When designing your text and labels, use plenty of white space (or other colored space as appropriate), images (either objects from the exhibition itself or elements that are drawn from objects in the exhibition), or other design devices (e.g., horizontal rules) to break up your text. Labels are often more effective if they are set off in a distinctive visual manner (different fonts, font color, font size) from the narrative exhibition text.

USING TEXT IMAGES

With the limitations on font types noted above, web designers are often tempted to use text images for their exhibitions. Text images, or bit-mapped text, are images created in an image program (e.g., Photoshop) that are simply pictures of letters and words. The benefit of text images is that they enable you as a designer to use all the fonts that are currently on your computer (or that you may purchase for the project). The downside of text images is that profligate use of them will dramatically slow down the loading of your page. Text images are of a fixed size (that of the image), and thus on monitors with varying resolutions the text will appear in varying sizes.

Though web usability guides generally frown on the use of text images for typical websites, for online exhibitions they are almost a necessity for achieving the best design.

This does not give designers carte blanche to create entire exhibitions with all the text in the form of bit-mapped images. As a general rule, use text images only for major headings within the exhibition, and always provide an "alt" attribute with the text of the image tag.

EXHIBITION NAVIGATION PRINCIPLES

In studies of web users it was found that most website visitors will delve no more deeply than a few pages into a site.[*] In an online exhibition, you will want to lure your visitors through the narrative theme that was developed in your script; provide them with thorough, informative, educational, and entertaining labels; and thrill them with images from your collections.

If the visitor clicks out of your site after only a single page or three, much of your work will have been for nothing. At the same time, your visitors will

---

*See, for example, Bernardo A. Huberman, Peter L. T. Pirolli, James E. Pitkow, and Rajan M. Lukose, "Strong Regularities in World Wide Web Searching," *Science* 280 (3 April 1998): 95–97.

not want to be scrolling through single, long pages of text. Fortunately, in the hypertext world of online exhibitions, such problems can be dealt with through use of effective design.

First, plan your design around principles that will allow you to break the narrative text and objects into discrete sections or components. This will allow you to create relatively small pages. Use a good sampling of effectively sized images and well-designed text blocks to create pages that work as a individual units. The object images may or may not have labels associated with them at this point (depending on the space available). If there is no space for a full label, you can provide a brief or truncated label that is sufficient to identify the object. Now here is where the hypertext capability of online exhibitions comes in handy. By using hyperlinks, you can show visitors a much larger image of the object and provide more extensive label text. You may want to provide even more information about the object. For books and manuscripts, you could provide text transcriptions, additional page or leaf openings, or alternative images of the object.

Next, you will want to design the online exhibition so that visitors can navigate through with some sort of structure. For gallery exhibitions, it has been noted that "once in the exhibition, visitors spend a disproportionate amount of their visit time near the entrance, and progressively less and less time on exhibits as they move towards the exit" (Belcher 1991, 112). Just as in gallery exhibitions, where visitors spend most of their time at the beginning, this exit gradient effect is exacerbated in an online exhibition for the reasons noted previously. Unlike in a physical exhibition, where the lure of a gift shop, a cafeteria, or even a rest room may at least draw visitors from point A to point B, in an online exhibition, there is always something else just a click away that can steal visitors from your exhibition.

For gallery exhibitions, a number of circulation patterns for visitors have been defined. These patterns are arterial, comb, chain, star/fan, and block (Belcher 1991, 114). In an arterial exhibition, the viewer is drawn through the exhibition in a fairly linear fashion from the beginning to the end. In a comb design, the central exhibition core is broken by side galleries. A chain design allows the visitor to circulate through a set pattern. A star/fan pattern has exhibits that fan out from a central core. And a block design basically allows the visitor to move through an unpatterned series of exhibits.

For an online exhibition, these design structures can be emulated. The easiest design to emulate is the arterial. In this type of design, the viewer will simply click through (forward and back) the items or pages in the exhibition. Given the advantages of hypertext, however, other patterns are often more popular for online exhibitions. An examination of a number of online exhibitions suggests that one popular navigation option roughly resembles the star/fan. In this type of online exhibition, once viewers enter, they are given a number of choices about how to proceed through the contents of the exhibition. After each choice, all the previous choices remain available in the form of menus or links on each page.

Granted the ability to offer viewers many paths through an online exhibition, a designer can sometimes become overwhelmed with possibilities and give viewers too many choices. Remember to keep in mind the narrative of the exhibition and how the overall theme fits into the design of the exhibition.

And thus, this becomes a good time to note . . .

Beware the Hyperlink!

The availability of hyperlinks has led to the proliferation of documents that hyperlink, cross-link, and back-link just because they can. Giving your visitors lots of choices within and outside of your exhibition is good but can too often lead to confusion. In the case of an online exhibition, remember to tell a story and build an experience. A proliferation of links to resources outside the exhibition (even to your own resources) will distract from the story that you are trying to tell. Unless it is highly relevant and important for your viewer to leave your site to go to another site, it is best to save your hyperlinks for the well-thought-out and perfectly organized webliography or reading list that will accompany your site.

CONTRACTING ONLINE EXHIBITION DESIGN WORK

In some instances, limitations of time, staff talents, and money will dictate that the best course of action is to contract out the complete design and production of an online exhibition. Intellectual control and, in most cases, the writing of the script will stay in-house.

A number of points need to be taken into consideration when contracting out web design. Technical specifications and site maintenance are the most important.

The specifications should include the version of HTML (or XHTML) preferred. Clearly state what level(s) of accessibility the site should maintain. Details for the size of images, color, and navigation schemes also need to be spelled out. You may also wish to have any logos or other navigational or graphical icons delivered in their native format (e.g., Photoshop PSD files or Adobe Illustrator files) in the event that you need to modify them later. Be careful that the web designer does not use technologies that you will not be able to run on your own site. If the designer uses streaming audio or video, you must have the capability of serving those products on your web server.

Things change! When you have contracted out web design work and you want to make a change of some sort, you must be able to perform site maintenance on the online exhibition. Make certain that any site peculiarities (such as directory structure and file-naming conventions) are well understood (and documented) so that when the inevitable time comes that someone on your staff will need to make a change, it will be a painless process.

See appendix E for a suggested timeline for contracted exhibition design.

METADATA FOR ONLINE EXHIBITIONS

Once you have designed and mounted your online exhibition, you will want to make sure that others can find it. If your library or archive has a web-accessible online catalog, be certain that you catalog your exhibitions and make them available through your catalog. Additionally, you will want to embed metadata in the opening pages of the exhibition to assist Internet search engines in finding and properly indexing them.

A popular scheme for metadata is the Dublin Core (NISO Standard Z39.85). Dublin Core provides an extensible set of fifteen descriptive elements that create access points to items. See appendix F for an example of Dublin Core from an online exhibition.

As many of the more popular Internet search engines do not index Dublin Core metadata, it is also good to add the standard descriptive metatags to the head of your document:

```
<META NAME = "Author" CONTENT = "xxx">

<META NAME = "Keywords" CONTENT = "xxx">

<META NAME = "Description" CONTENT= "xxx">
```

QUICK TIPS FOR DESIGN

- If you are retrofitting a gallery exhibition, keep in mind that online and gallery exhibitions have different needs in design.
- Look at your design with a number of different screen resolutions.
- Try different color settings to see what happens to your design.
- Use many different browsers (and release versions of browsers) to look at your design.
- Don't forget to look at the design with a Mac (if designing with a PC).
- Don't forget to look at the design with a PC (if designing with a Mac).
- Change the default font and screen colors on your browser and see what happens to your design.
- Carefully select your fonts for headings and text to ensure that they will be legible.
- Use text images sparingly and for maximum effect.
- Considering that users may wish to print portions of your exhibition (e.g., bibliographies), design appropriate or alternative pages suitable for printing.
- Choose an appropriate navigation scheme for the narrative of your exhibition.
- User hyperlinks judiciously.
- Provide metadata access points to your exhibition.

SOURCES CITED

Archer, Bruce. 1965. *Systematic Method for Designers*. London: Council of Industrial Design.

Earnshaw, Simon. 1997. "Typography on the Web." Available at: http://msdn.microsoft.com/workshop/design/type/typography.asp.

Gillespie, Joe. 2000. "Typography." Web Page Design for Designers. Available at: http://www.wpdfd.com/wpdtypo.htm.

Goode, George Brown. 1891. "The Museums of the Future." In *Annual Report of the Board of Regents of the Smithsonian Institution for the Year Ending June 30, 1889*, pp. 427–445. Washington, D.C.: GPO.

Jacobi, Daniel, and Marie Sylvie Poli. 1995. "Scriptovisual Documents in Exhibitions: Some Theoretical Guidelines." In *Text in the Exhibition Medium*, ed. Andrée Blais, pp. 49–78. Montreal: Société des musées québécois: Musée de la Civilisation.

Merchant, David. 2000. "The Trouble with Color." *Library Computing* 18, no. 3: 208–212.

Optimizing Web Graphics. 28 February 2000. Available at: http://www. webreference.com/dev/graphics/index.html.

Pierroux, Palmyre. "Art in Networks: Information and Communication Technology in Art Museums." Available at: http://www.media.uio.no/ internettiendring/publikasjoner/tekst/Pierroux/02Contents.html.

Smithsonian Institution Libraries. *Voyages: A Smithsonian Libraries' Exhibition.* Available at: http://www.sil.si.edu/Exhibitions/Voyages.

Spencer, J., and L. Reynolds. 1977. *Directional Signing and Labelling in Libraries and Museums: A Review of Current Theory and Practice,* p. 100. London: Readability of Print Unit, Royal College of Art. Quoted in Michael Belcher, Exhibitions in Museums (Washington, D.C.: Smithsonian Institution Press, 1991).

Strizver, Ilene. 2001. *Type Rules!* Cincinnati: North Light.

OTHER WEBSITES DISCUSSED

The Browser-Safe Color Palette. By Lynda Weinman.
http://www.lynda.com/hex.html

CGSD Gamma page.
http://www.cgsd.com/papers/gamma.html

Color Matters.
http://www.colormatters.com

"Color My World." By Molly E. Holzschlag. Web Techniques.
http://www. webtechniques.com/archives/2000/09/desi

Dublin Core Home Page.
http://www.dublincore.org

Frequently Asked Questions about Fonts. The comp.fonts FAQ, Version 2.1.5., 14 August 1996. Compiled by Norman Walsh.
http://www.nwalsh.com/comp.fonts/FAQ/index.html

Netscape Color Names.
http://developer.netscape.com/docs/manuals/htmlguid/colortab.htm; also http://www.tanega.com/java/color3.html

"Typography on the Web." By Frank Boumphrey.
http://www.hypermedic.com/style/typog/typindex.htm

Web Page Design for Designers. Browsergrid.
http://www.wpdfd.com/browsergrid.htm

"Why Do Images Appear Darker on Some Displays? An Explanation of Monitor Gamma." By Robert W. Berger.
http://www.vtiscan.com/~rwb/gamma.html

CHAPTER
9

Online Exhibitions
Case Studies and Awards

In addition to the reward of having many visitors to our online exhibitions, it is always nice to get an award! First let's look at some elements of online exhibitions and then at some of the awards that are currently available for online exhibitions.

CASE STUDIES

To analyze how libraries and archives have put together online exhibitions, let's look at some case studies. We will view exhibitions in the following categories:

> Use of book materials
>
> Use of archival materials
>
> Techno-gizmo sites
>
> Retrospective conversion of gallery exhibitions to online exhibitions

Use of Book Materials

An online exhibition of books differs from, say, an online exhibition devoted to dinosaur bones or airplanes. One important difference is that when using books, we experience them primarily as two-dimensional objects. Though we hold a book in our hands, move it around, view the top edge, sides, and so forth, our primary contact with the actual object is to view, read, and interact with the text or illustrations on the page.

There are, though, obvious exceptions to this use of a book: the fine bindings that we need to see all parts of, the pop-up book that needs to be handled and viewed from various angles, and the artist's book that exists more as an object than as an item of use.

At its most simple, an online exhibition of book material will present the book and relevant information about it. From McGill University Libraries comes *Bibliotheca Canadiana. A Historical Survey of Canadian Bibliography / Étude Historique de la Bibliographie Canadienne* (see figure 17). For this exhibition, the curator has chosen works that trace "the development of Canadian bibliography from the early eighteenth century to the late twentieth century." Each book in the exhibition is represented by a single image and includes a full bibliographic citation and a brief contextual label. A similar exhibition, *Birds!*

FIGURE 17 | *Bibliotheca Canadiana. A Historical Survey of Canadian Bibliography / Étude Historique de la Bibliographie Canadienne.* Rare Books and Special Collections Division, McGill University Libraries, Montreal, Canada.

from the National Library of Australia, presents plates from numerous works illustrating birds. The plates are, in many cases, cropped to show the portion of the page on which the bird appears. A third example, *From Alchemy to Chemistry: Five Hundred Years of Rare and Interesting Books*, from the University of Illinois at Urbana-Champaign, Rare Book and Special Collections Library, includes extensive notes on each work as well as more than one view of it.

Use of Archival Materials

Much like library online exhibitions, archival online exhibitions will focus on two-dimensional objects. In many cases, archives will have additional material in their exhibitions (such as photographs), but the focus will likely remain two-dimensional.

From the Nova Scotia Archives and Records Management office comes *Halifax and Its People / 1749–1999* (see figure 18). This exhibition consists of photographs, prints, maps, and other material in the archives relating to the people of Halifax. Introducing various legal documents and manuscripts to the exhibition process, the Utah State Archives, in *Utah's Road to Statehood,* uses small, excerpted images that click to larger versions of the original materials.

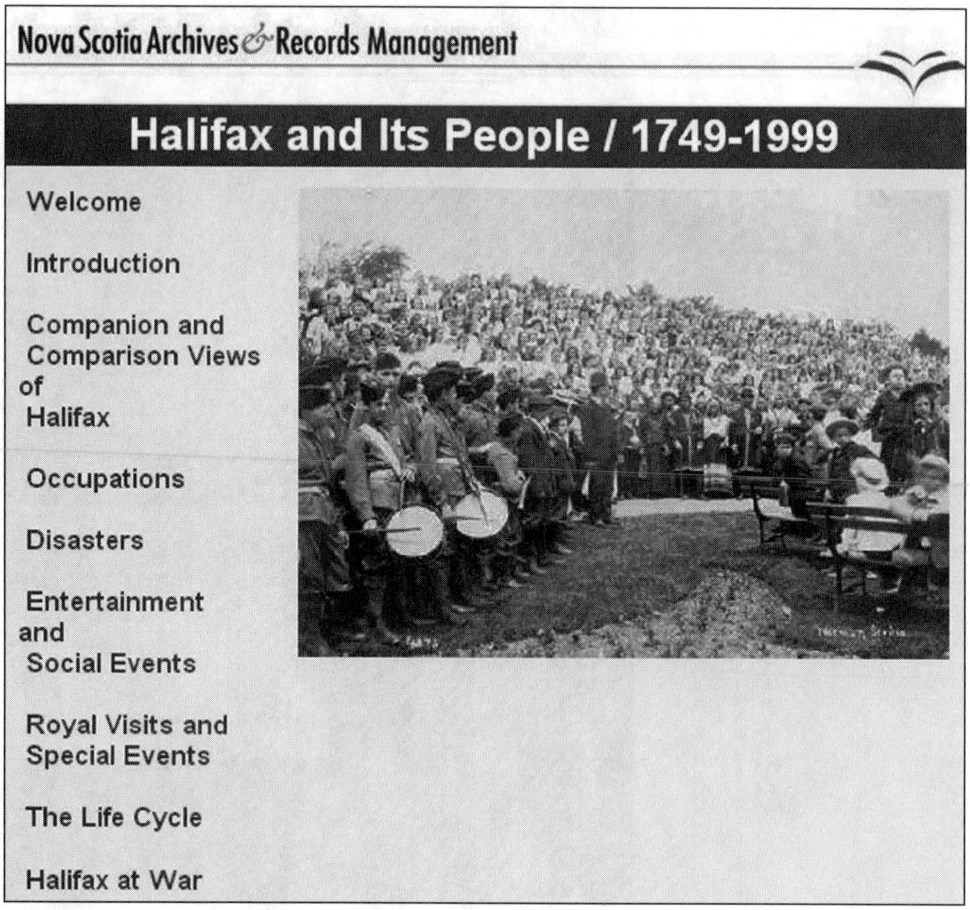

Nova Scotia Archives & Records Management

Halifax and Its People / 1749-1999

Welcome

Introduction

Companion and
Comparison Views
of
Halifax

Occupations

Disasters

Entertainment
and
Social Events

Royal Visits and
Special Events

The Life Cycle

Halifax at War

FIGURE 18 | *Halifax and Its People, 1749–1999.* Nova Scotia Archives and Records Management, N-0337.

Many archives include oral histories in their collections. When transcripts are available, it is often a benefit to viewers of the exhibition to be able to link to the full transcript. Additionally, audio technology will enable users to listen to digitized audio tracks from recorded oral histories. This technology is used in the exhibition *Lee Wilson and Company Archives,* from the University of Arkansas.

Techno-Gizmo Sites

Once multimedia in the form of audio is introduced into an online exhibition, it's only a short step to offering even more complex multimedia experiences for the exhibition viewer. An extremely complex (and sometimes confusing) navigation is used by the United States Holocaust Memorial Museum in the exhibition entitled *Do You Remember, When.* This exhibition uses multiple layers of diary pages and other archival materials to tell the story of Manfred Lewin, a young Jew living in Nazi Berlin in 1941. The manner in which the original artifacts (in this case, two-dimensional diary pages) are presented—with a page-turning navigation scheme, overlaid translations, and commentary—would be difficult to accomplish in a gallery exhibition (see figure 19).

An interesting use of Flash technology is evident in *The Edible Monument: The Art of Food for Festivals,* from the Getty Research Institute. The Flash

UNITED STATES HOLOCAUST MEMORIAL MUSEUM

TURN   PAGE

Translation

To understand why Manfred Lewin,
a young Jew in Nazi Berlin,
wrote this book in 1941

for his friend Gad Beck
- to understand why Gad, 19 and Jewish,
risked his life attempting to save Manfred
from deportation - read these words from
the play that brought them together. German
writer Friedrich von Schiller's Don Carlos:

No matter what you plan on doing, will you promise
To undertake no act without your friend?
Will you make me this promise?

Friendship, valor, and the fight for freedom were the ideals of this 18th
-century German drama. In 1941, Gad and Manfred played the starring roles in their Jewish
youth group's reading of the play

FIGURE 19 | *Do You Remember, When.* United States Holocaust Memorial Museum.

animation provides an excellent introduction to this exhibition of architectural food fantasies. Using illustrations from cookbooks and other food-oriented books and prints from the sixteenth through nineteenth centuries, the curators trace the history of ornate edible architecture and sculptures.

One of the most complex online exhibitions originating in a library or archive is *Writing on Hands: Memory and Knowledge in Early Modern Europe*, from Dickinson College, in collaboration with the Folger Shakespeare Library. This exhibition is organized around six themes that "concern the learning, ordering, and recollection of abstract concepts related to human experience and culture." Making the exhibition more interactive are a collection of Flash animations, Java applets, and other devices that let the viewer interact with the objects. An example is an illustration of a fifteenth-century woodcut of a human hand covered in musical notations. By clicking on various parts of the hand, the viewer is able to listen to the associated musical note.

Retrospective Conversion of Gallery Exhibitions to Online Exhibitions

As mentioned in chapter 8, in many cases, you will want to take advantage of work done in earlier gallery exhibitions and convert them to online exhibitions. *Women's Bodies, Women's Property: Limited Ownership under the Law: German Common-Law Books Illustrated in the Fourteenth Century*, from Tufts University Archives and Special Collections, is an example of such a converted exhibition. As noted in the introduction to the online version: "The web version of the original exhibit was prepared by the Tufts University archives in January 1999. This version attempts, as far as possible, to recreate the order of the original exhibit panels as they were mounted in the Slater Concourse. Other material explaining the origins of the law books and other background information was originally displayed in cases in the lobby of the gallery. This information has been formatted for the web."

Going back even further into their exhibition archives, the Glasgow University Library's Special Collections created *The Damned Art: An Exhibition of Books Relating to the History of Witchcraft and Demonology* in 1999 from an exhibition originally held in their gallery in 1985. A third example of a retro-converted exhibition, done shortly after the gallery exhibition, is *Science and the Artist's Book,* from Smithsonian Institution Libraries.

AWARDS FOR ONLINE EXHIBITIONS

The RBMS Awards

Well, now that you've gone through all that work, what else, besides satisfaction, will you get? Awards! Honors! Fame! Well, maybe at least two out of three.

The Rare Book and Manuscripts Section (RBMS) of the Association of College and Research Libraries Division of the American Library Association began presenting awards for online exhibitions in 2001. The award for online exhibitions is an outgrowth of the award that RBMS has been giving for printed exhibition catalogs since 1986.

The Katharine Kyes Leab and Daniel J. Leab *American Book Prices* Current Exhibition Awards are given for "excellence in the publication of catalogs and brochures that accompany exhibitions of library and archival materials, as well as for electronic versions of such materials."

The RBMS Guidelines and Rules for Submissions state:

> The judging of electronic exhibitions is a three-year pilot project beginning with the 2001 Awards period. Electronic exhibitions submitted for consideration must be sponsored by a library or archival institution. Eligibility is extended both to electronic exhibitions created as representations of physically existing exhibitions, as well as to "virtual" exhibitions existing only in an electronic format. Entrants in this category may be commended for overall excellence in design, concept, informational value, and navigability. . . . Electronic library and archival exhibitions are limited to those with stable URL addresses.

In 2001, the joint winners of the Leab award were *Nabokov under Glass: A Centennial Exhibition,* from the the Henry W. and Albert A. Berg Collection of English and American Literature, Humanities and Social Sciences Library, New York Public Library (see figure 20), and *Bridging the Bay: Bridging the Campus,* from the University of California, Berkeley, Water Resources Center Archives and Environmental Design Archives.

Further information on the award and the nomination and judging criteria can be found at the RBMS website. For a list of nominees and winners of the 2001 award, see appendix G.

Museums and the Web: Best Online Exhibition or Activity Site Award

Another major award for online exhibitions comes from Museums and the Web, sponsored by Archives and Museum Informatics.

This award is open to a wide variety of institutions. The organization focuses on museums, but archives and libraries are very welcome to nominate their online exhibitions for the award.

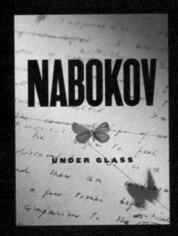

NABOKOV
UNDER GLASS

This website is based on an exhibition, of the same name, drawn from the Vladimir Nabokov Archive of the Henry W. and Albert A. Berg Collection of English and American Literature, and presented on the occasion of the centennial of the writer's birth.

"... the first part of my life is marked by a rather pleasing chronological neatness. I spent my first twenty years in Russia, the next twenty in Western Europe, and the twenty years after that, from 1940 to 1960, in America. I've been living in Europe again for five years now, but I cannot promise to stay around another fifteen so as to retain the rhythm."
Vladimir Nabokov, in a 1965 interview

ENTER

FIGURE 20 | *Nabokov under Glass.* Henry W. and Albert A. Berg Collection of English and American Literature, Humanities and Social Sciences Library, New York Public Library.

The award Best Online Exhibition or Activity Site has been given since 1997. In addition to online exhibitions, Museums and the Web presents a number of other awards for museum-related sites. According to the organization's website:

These sites excelled in presenting and interpreting museum collections and themes, providing a rich and meaningful virtual experience. They may have been a section of a larger museum web or a collaborative project between institutions and/or individuals and communities associated with museums. Entirely virtual museums were eligible to participate in this category as were exhibitions of web art and other "born digital" collections. Quality characteristics include:

Effective use of multiple media formats

Innovative ways of complementing physical exhibitions or providing surrogates for physical experiences in online-only exhibitions

New ways of representing museum processes and structures

Imaginative audience participation and engagement of different categories of "visitors"

The award winner in 2001 was *Tempus Fugit: Time Flies,* from the Nelson-Atkins Museum of Art. This complex exhibition from the museum focuses on the nature of time and how it has been portrayed in art over the years. One judge, commenting on the selection of this site as the winner, noted, "My first choice here is the Tempus Fugit site as it's a strong total package: lovely design, strong content that is thoughtfully conceived and well executed throughout."

SOURCES CITED

"Best Online Exhibition or Activity Site." Museums and the Web 2001. Available at: http://www.archimuse.com/mw2001/best/virtual.html.

"Best Online Exhibition or Activity Site [Winner]." Museums and the Web 2001. Available at: http://www.archimuse.com/mw2001/best/win_virtual.html.

RBMS. Guidelines and Rules for Submissions. Available at: http://www.rbms.nd.edu/committees/exhibition_awards/submissions/rules.shtml.

ONLINE EXHIBITIONS DISCUSSED

Bibliotheca Canadiana. A Historical Survey of Canadian Bibliography / Étude Historique de la Bibliographie Canadienne. Rare Books and Special Collections Division, McGill University Libraries.
http://www.library.mcgill.ca/rarebook/bibcanho.htm

Birds! National Library of Australia. http://www.nla.gov.au/exhibitions/birds

Bridging the Bay: Bridging the Campus. University of California, Berkeley, Water Resources Center Archives and Environmental Design Archives.
http://www.lib.berkeley.edu/Exhibits/Bridge

The Damned Art: An Exhibition of Books Relating to the History of Witchcraft and Demonology. Glasgow University Library, Special Collections.
http://special.lib.gla.ac.uk/exhibns/damnedart/index.html

Do You Remember, When. United States Holocaust Memorial Museum.
http://www.ushmm.org/doyourememberwhen/index.htm

The Edible Monument: The Art of Food for Festivals. Getty Research Institute.
http://www.getty.edu/gri/exhibit/ediblemonument

From Alchemy to Chemistry: Five Hundred Years of Rare and Interesting Books. University of Illinois at Urbana-Champaign, Rare Book and Special Collections Library.
http://www.scs.uiuc.edu/~mainzv/exhibit/index.htm

Halifax and Its People / 1749–1999. Nova Scotia Archives and Records Management.
http://www.gov.ns.ca/nsarm/virtualx/halifax

Lee Wilson and Company Archives. University of Arkansas.
http://www.uark.edu/misc/ardiglib/leewilson/index.html

Nabokov under Glass: A Centennial Exhibition. Henry W. and Albert A. Berg Collection of English and American Literature, Humanities and Social Sciences Library, New York Public Library.
http://www.nypl.org/research/chss/epo/nabokov

Science and the Artist's Book. Smithsonian Institution Libraries.
http://www.sil.si.edu/Exhibitions/Science-and-the-Artists-Book

Tempus Fugit: Time Flies. Nelson-Atkins Museum of Art.
http://www.nelson-atkins.org/tempusfugit

Utah's Road to Statehood. Utah State Archives.
http://www.archives.state.ut.us/exhibits/Statehood/setroad.htm

Women's Bodies, Women's Property: Limited Ownership under the Law: German Common-Law Books Illustrated in the Fourteenth Century. Tufts University Archives and Special Collections.
http://www.library.tufts.edu/archives/Exhibits/Law/tulips.html

Writing on Hands: Memory and Knowledge in Early Modern Europe. Dickinson College, in collaboration with the Folger Shakespeare Library.
http://www.writingonhands.org

OTHER WEBSITES DISCUSSED

Museums and the Web.
http://www.archimuse.com/conferences/mw.html

Rare Book and Manuscripts Section Home Page.
http://www.rbms.nd.edu

CHAPTER 10

Conclusion
Online With the Show!

THE PERILS AND JOYS OF A LARGE AUDIENCE

Online exhibitions enable libraries and archives to present images from their collections to a wider audience. As more and more first-cut research is being done on the Web, a well-designed online exhibition can provide many users with a good introduction to a complex subject.

Other surprise benefits may accrue to unexpected visitors stumbling on your exhibition. An advertising designer, browsing the Web, visited one the Smithsonian Institution Libraries' online exhibitions and found the perfect image to use in an advertisement.

In a now aging survey of museum websites, Jonathan P. Bowen (1999) noted the following facts:

Eighty-eight percent of visitors to museum web pages are based in North America.

Forty-six percent of virtual museum visitors are women.

The average age of people visiting museum web pages is between forty and sixty-four years.

Seventy-four percent of visitors expect to find online exhibitions.

Eighty-seven percent expect to find images and fifty-two percent expect to be able to download images

For libraries and archives hoping to capture the teen or non-U.S. market, these statistics are not heartening. Likewise, curators who wish to keep tight control over images from their collections will not be pleased to know that over half of the visitors hope to download images.

Another fear often expressed, but not borne out in any formal study, is that when images from a collection are made available, especially in the form of an accessible online exhibition, visitors will flock to the library, archive, or museum and overwhelm staff with requests to see the original books, manuscripts, or artifacts. Though libraries, archives, and museums are unlikely to increase their staffing to deal with expanded patronage, these memory institutions need to encourage greater use and not thwart it! Electronic dissemination of their contents, particularly in the form of online exhibitions, is a perfect way to do so.

An increasingly wired world makes even the most distant parts of the globe local. Libraries, archives, and museums need to bring their collections to the fore and make them a more important part of the global information community. As Lester Asheim (1987, 19) has noted, "Exposure to any form of communications is like any other kind of educational experience; deeper involvement in it carries a wider range of satisfactions for those who learn from their experience to probe more deeply and more widely into the capacity of the medium to convey different levels of content."

As experience with creating online exhibitions grows within your institution, the experience for both the creators and the viewers will deepen and become enriched. So, online with the show!

SOURCES CITED

Asheim, Lester. 1987. *The Reader, Viewer, Listener: An Essay in Communication.* Washington, D.C.: Library of Congress.

Bowen, Jonathan P. 1999. "Time for Renovations: A Survey of Museum Web Sites." Museums and the Web 1999. Available at: http://www.museums.reading.ac.uk/mw99/paper.

Sample Online Exhibition Proposal

Nile Notes of a Howadji:
American Travelers in Egypt, 1837 to 1901
by Martin R. Kalfatovic

Exhibition Overview

Travel literature is an increasingly popular research tool for anthropologists and natural and social historians, as well as an informative and entertaining resource for the armchair traveler. Egypt has been a popular destination for travelers from the time of Herodotus to the present, and Americans have been visiting Egypt since the beginning of the nineteenth century.

Americans' travel accounts were markedly different from those of their European counterparts, displaying a certain brashness and a paradoxical tendency to praise Egypt for not being like Europe and to criticize it for not being enough like the United States. The works selected for the exhibition will focus on the American experience in Egypt and how it was expressed in travel literature.

The proposed title of the exhibition is drawn from the title of George W. Curtis's 1851 account of his travels to Egypt, *Nile Notes of a Howadji*. Curtis, among other things, an editor of *Harper's Magazine,* wrote an interesting account that was frequently cited by later travelers. Howadji, a Turkish term originally meaning merchant, soon came to mean a traveler of any kind and, eventually, a tourist, and was commonly used throughout the areas of Turkish influence.

The exhibition will be organized around three sections:

Early travel (from the first American visitor to Egypt, circa 1810, to approximately 1870, when travel became more popular and Egypt became just another stop on the "Grand Tour"). Travelers in this section include John Lloyd Stephens, Bayard Taylor, William C. Prime, and G. F. Train.

Travel guides, tour books, maps, and the like; the "helper" literature of the traveler (Smithsonian Institution Libraries holds a good collection of this type of material, including early Baedekers).

The "American on Tour" (from approximately 1870 to 1914—the beginning of the First World War, after which the political status of Egypt was dramatically changed); this section will focus more on the tourist in Egypt, including some of the well-known figures that went (Mark Twain, Andrew Carnegie, U. S. Grant—called the Emperor of America in Egypt—and the actress Maude Adams) as well as the average American traveler.

Historical and theoretical research for this exhibition is based on the curator's book, *Nile Notes of a Howadji: Travelers' Tales from Egypt, Antiquity through 1918* (Scarecrow Press, 1992), and a paper, "Nile Notes of a Howadji: American Travellers in Egypt, 1837–1910," presented at St. Catherine's College, Oxford, at the conference "Travellers in Egypt and the Near East" in July 1997.

Book and periodical material would be drawn from a number of the Libraries' collections, including the National Museum of African Art, Anthropology, the National Museum of American History, the Annex facility, and the Natural History Museum.

Supplemental materials drawn from other Smithsonian collections would include portraits of selected travelers, a map of the Nile with commonly visited locales highlighted, selected color photographs of contemporary Egypt, and artifacts (where appropriate). Historical black-and-white photographs of travelers to Egypt from the National Anthropological Archive (Natural History) will also be used.

Projected Audience

The primary audience for this exhibition will be those interested in historical travel to Egypt. Narrative and labels will be written for an informed audience who will have some background knowledge of this topic. Members of the Association for the Study of Travel in Egypt and the Near East would be a logical audience for this exhibition.

Design

The online design for this exhibition is envisioned to include references to Egypt. Deep reds and blues and fonts appropriate to the period may be used to evoke travel to Egypt in the nineteenth century. Layout will be roughly chronological for the two travelers' sections and object-oriented for the section on supplemental travel material. Portraits, contemporary images, and historical photographs will also be used in the exhibition. Additional materials such as a bibliography will be included.

Maintenance

This is envisioned as a static exhibition that will not be updated further.

Staff

Staff requested for this exhibition includes approximately five hours of time of a selected staff person for proofreading final text. No additional staff time outside of Exhibits Team work will be needed.

Budget

No additional budget requests are foreseen for this project.

Projected Timeline

Script begun	Week 1
First draft of script complete	Week 4
Digitizing images used for exhibition	Weeks 3–4
Image preparation	Week 5
Final draft of script approved	Weeks 5–6
Design and layout planning	Weeks 4–6
Page markup	Week 7
Final proofing of pages	Week 8
Exhibition goes live	Week 9

Preliminary Object List

Approximately twenty-five books will be used in this exhibition; multiple page openings (and/or cover shots) will be used for some objects. See attached list [not included in this sample].

Sample Exhibition Script

The text below is excerpted from the exhibition script for *Frontier Photographer: Edward S. Curtis,* by William Baxter of Smithsonian Institution Libraries. It is reproduced with permission.

*****

Title

Frontier Photographer: Edward S. Curtis
A Smithsonian Institution Libraries Exhibition

#

Superquote

"Take a good look. We're not going to see this kind of thing much longer. It already belongs to the past."
—George Bird Grinnell to Edward S. Curtis, referring to the Sun Dance gathering of Blackfeet, Algonquin, and Bloods in 1900

#

Canyon de Chelly image

This image of the Canyon de Chelly in Arizona is perhaps the best known of Edward S. Curtis' photogravure prints.

Canyon de Chelly, by Edward S. Curtis, 1904.
Lent by Secretary and Mrs. I. Michael Heyman.

#

Introductory text

The Legacy of Edward S. Curtis
"I regard the work you do as one of the most valuable works which any American could now do."
—President Theodore Roosevelt in a letter to Edward S. Curtis, Dec. 16, 1905

Edward S. Curtis (1868–1952) left an indelible mark on the history of photography in his 20-volume life's work, *The North American Indian.*

Part photographic essay, part ethnographic survey, and part work of art, Curtis' North American Indian Project represented an attempt to capture images of American Indians as they lived before contact with Anglo cultures. The photogravure prints in *The North American Indian* reveal peoples whose traditional ways of life were coming to an end as the U.S. frontier began to fade.

Thirty years of grueling work on the North American Indian Project cost the artist his marriage and his health. It also yielded an American legacy that is an artistic masterpiece.

#

Opening image

"Three Chiefs—Piegan," from portfolio of *The North American Indian,* Vol. VI, 1911.

#

Curtis and Guptil advertisement	"One of the greatest examples of business energy and perseverance to be found in Seattle today." —*Argus* magazine, Dec. 14, 1896 Advertisement extolling Curtis and Guptil Studio, one of Curtis' earliest photographic ventures.

SECTION 1 (Introducing Curtis, His Family)

Superquote	"If you hear anyone say I am not to succeed tell them they don't know me." —Edward S. Curtis in a letter to his friend Edmond Meany, about 1908 #
Subhead: **Home Life**	"He became determined to escape from his father's world, from a life of grinding physical labor and failure. He was going to . . . make something of himself." —An unnamed relative describing Edward S. Curtis, date unknown "We always said he had no home life at all." —Florence Curtis Graybill
Visual and label: **Edward S. Curtis** **Clara Curtis with** **Beth, Harold, and** **Florence**	"Bright, well-read, a good conversationalist. [Clara, Edward's wife] shared Edward's love for this great, scenic land of the Northwest—but not his interest in photography." —An unnamed relative, about 1900 Born in 1868 in Whitewater, Wisconsin, Edward S. Curtis grew up in poverty. His father was in ill health and never fully able to support the family. After his father died, Edward took a series of odd jobs, ultimately settling on photography as a career. He taught himself from books and even made his own camera. When Edward Curtis married Clara Phillips in 1892, she joined him in his increasingly successful Seattle studio. They had four children. Ultimately, as Curtis worked on *The North American Indian,* his long absences and infrequent financial support led to a bitter divorce. Curtis' children nonetheless remained loyal and active supporters until his death in 1952. Edward S. Curtis, by unknown artist, about 1890. Courtesy James Graybill, Edward S. Curtis' grandson. Clara Phillips Curtis, wife of Edward S. Curtis, and three of their children: Beth, Harold, and Florence, probably by Edward S. Curtis, date unknown. Courtesy James Graybill, Edward S. Curtis' grandson.
Superquote	"I have made about every sacrifice a human being can for the sake of the work, and the work is worth it. . . . The lack of comparatively paltry dollars is maddening." —Edward S. Curtis in a letter to J. P. Morgan's office, 1913 #

Subhead:

Who Was Edward S. Curtis?

"Try to make your work show some individuality . . . make it look yourself; let it show that you have put part of your life into it."
—Edward S. Curtis, *The Western Trail,* Seattle, 1900

Edward S. Curtis

"Daughters of well-to-do families . . . believed that having their portraits made by Edward Curtis . . . gave them glamor."
—Florence Curtis Graybill, 1977

At a time when photographers were struggling to establish photography as a legitimate art form, Curtis' work was already being hailed for its artistic merits. Curtis saw himself as an artist with a mission.

Self-portrait, by Edward S. Curtis, about 1899.
Courtesy James Graybill, Edward S. Curtis' grandson.

MAP OF NORTH AMERICA

Map label:

Mapping Curtis' Accomplishments

In the 30 years it took to complete the North American Indian Project, Curtis visited almost 100 Indian tribes in the western third of the United States and Alaska. Although he fell short of his ideal of visiting all of the North American tribes—which may have numbered in the thousands—his was nonetheless an awesome accomplishment. In an era when domestic travel involved risk and uncertainty, he managed, through careful planning and tenacity, to cover 40,000 miles of western terrain by rail, by waterway, by foot, and by any other means he could find.

#

Guidelines for Reproducing Works from Exhibition Websites

Generally, a list of guidelines for reproducing works from your collections will include a statement that the images may be used for personal or research use. For those that wish to use the images for commercial purposes, it is best to lay out your institution's general principles for that type of use and, most importantly, direct them to where they can get that type of permission.

Below are a few examples of use policies.

American Museum of Natural History / Copyright

All text, images, and software on this website are copyright property of the American Museum of Natural History and its programmers unless otherwise noted. They may be used for the personal education of website visitors. They may not be placed in the public domain. Any commercial reproduction, redistribution, publication, or other use by electronic means or otherwise is prohibited unless pursuant to a written license signed by the Museum.

http://www.amnh.org/common/copyright

Cornel University / Permission to Publish

Users of the collections are expected to abide by all copyright laws. Photocopies and other reproductions are provided for research use only and may not be transferred or recopied without permission. Materials from the collections cannot be published without obtaining the legally required permission. Permission requests should be directed to Permissions Coordinator, Division of Rare and Manuscript Collections, 2B Carl A. Kroch Library, Cornell University, Ithaca, NY, 14853. Permission requests should include: title of publication, expected date of publication, type of publication (scholarly, general, etc.) and expected print run or distribution. We will then review the request and respond regarding the permission and publication fee. In many cases, the Division of Rare and Manuscript Collections is owner of the physical object only. It is the obligation of the researcher to fulfill the requirements of the copyright law.

http://rmc.library.cornell.edu/services/repro.htm

Library of Congress / American Memory, Copyright, and Other Restrictions

The Library is offering broad public access to American Memory collections as a contribution to education and scholarship. Some materials in these collections may be protected by the U.S. Copyright Law (Title 17, U.S.C.) and/or by the copyright or neighboring-rights laws of other nations. More information about U.S. Copyright is provided by the Copyright Office. Additionally, the reproduction of some materials may be restricted by terms of Library of Congress gift or purchase agreements, donor restrictions, privacy and publicity rights, licensing, and trademarks.

Transmission or reproduction of protected items beyond that allowed by fair use requires the written permission of the copyright owners.

The nature of historical archival collections means that copyright or other information about restrictions may be difficult or even impossible to determine. Whenever possible, the Library provides information about copyright owners and other restrictions in the catalog records, finding aids, special-program illustration captions, and other texts that accompany collections. The Library provides such information as a service to aid patrons in determining the appropriate use of an item, but that determination ultimately rests with the patron.

As a publicly supported institution the Library generally does not own rights to material in its collections. Therefore, it does not charge permission fees for use of such material and cannot give or deny permission to publish or otherwise distribute material in its collections. It is the patron's obligation to determine and satisfy copyright or other use restrictions when publishing or otherwise distributing materials found in the Library's collections.

The Library of Congress is eager to hear from any copyright owners who are not properly identified so that appropriate information may be provided in the future.

http://lcweb2.loc.gov/ammem/copyrit2.html

Metropolitan Museum of Art / Terms and Conditions [excerpt]

Access to and use of the Metropolitan Museum of Art's image and text files and data on this site are subject to the following terms and conditions:

1. The text, images, and data on The Metropolitan Museum of Art (the "Museum") Web site (the "Site") are protected by copyright and may be covered by other restrictions as well. The Museum retains all rights, including copyright, in data, images, software, documentation, text, and other information contained in these files (collectively, the "Materials"). Copyright and other proprietary rights may be held by individuals or entities other than, or in addition to, the Museum.

2. The Materials are made available for limited non-commercial, educational, and personal use only, or for fair use as defined in the United States copyright laws. Users may download these files for their own use, subject to any additional terms or restrictions which may be applicable to the individual file or program. Users must, however, cite the author and source of the Materials as they would material from any printed work, and the citations should include the URL "www.metmuseum.org."

http://www.metmuseum.org/copyright.htm

National Archives and Records Administration / Copyright, Restrictions, and Permissions Notice [excerpt]

Generally, materials produced by Federal agencies are in the public domain and may be reproduced without permission. However, not all materials appearing on this website are in the public domain. Some materials have been donated or obtained from individuals or organizations and may be subject to restrictions on use.

http://www.nara.gov/nara/terms.html#copyright

National Gallery of Art / Conditions of Use

The contents of this site, including all images and text, are for personal, educational, non-commercial use only. The contents of this site may not be reproduced in any form without the permission of the National Gallery of Art.

http://www.nga.gov/copyright/copy.htm

New York Public Library / Guidelines for Using Images and Text from The New York Public Library

As part of its public service mission, The New York Public Library provides reproductions of certain items from its collections, for PERSONAL or RESEARCH USE ONLY. Any other use, including but not limited to commercial or scholarly publication, exhibition, online/web site, broadcast/film, home video, and promotional use without prior written permission of the Library is strictly prohibited.

Granting or withholding of permission is determined by the Library on a case by case basis, and a usage fee is required.

Users should be aware that materials made available directly through the divisions and through this web site may be subject to additional restrictions including but not limited to copyright and the rights of privacy and publicity, of parties other than the Library. USERS ARE SOLELY RESPONSIBLE for determining the existence of such rights and for obtaining any other permissions, and paying associated fees, which may be necessary for the proposed use.

http://www.nypl.org/admin/pro/copies

Smithsonian Institution / Rules and Conditions For Using Smithsonian Image Files [excerpt]

The Smithsonian Institution ("SI"), and its Office of Printing & Photographic Services ("OPPS") image files are made available for non-commercial, personal use. Copying or redistribution in any manner for personal or corporate gain is not permitted. SI specifically retains any rights, including possible copyright, which it may have in data, files, and/or the images they contain.

http://www.si.edu/siphotos/CAPTIONS/oppsrules.html

University of Virginia / Use and Reproduction of Materials

The materials on this website have been made available for use in research, teaching, and private study. For these purposes, you may reproduce (print, make photocopies, or download) materials from this website without prior permission, on the condition that you provide proper attribution of the source in all copies (see below).

Although we do not require you to contact us in advance for these purposes, we do appreciate hearing from teachers, students, and researchers who are using our resources in interesting ways (send e-mail to the Director of the Special Collections Digital Center at scdc@virginia.edu).

For other uses of materials from Special Collections—i.e., commercial products, print publication, broadcast, mirroring, reuse on a website, and anything else that does not fall under "fair use" (explained below)—we require that you contact us in advance for permission to reproduce our materials.

The Special Collections Department reserves the right to refuse to accept a duplication request if, in its judgment, fulfillment of the request would involve violation of copyright law.

http://www.lib.virginia.edu/speccol/about/use.html

APPENDIX

D

Suggested Database Structure for Online Exhibitions

ID Field	
item_id	Generally a required field in a database to uniquely identify items.

Author/Creator Information	
author_last	Author last name.
author_first	Author first name.
author_dates	Life dates of author.
other_authors	Include in this field other authors of the item in a standardized format.

Item Information	
title	Title of the item.
title_translation	Translation of the title (into English or use for alternative language access to the object).
article_title	For nonbook or manuscript items, you may want to include an "article" field that could be formatted within quotation marks instead of in italics.
issue_information	For articles, you should include issue (volume, number, etc.) information.

Publication Information	
publisher	Publisher of the item.
publication_place	Place of publication.
publication_date	Date of publication.

Exhibition Information	
label	The text label that will accompany the object. Depending on the database system you use, you will want to make this field able to contain a great deal of text. For increased formatting capabilities, you may also be able to include standard HTML tags around the text in this field.
credit	The credit line that will accompany this item.
exhibition_section	If your exhibition will have a number of sections or parts, indicate in the database what section this item will fall into.
exhibition_subsection	If your exhibition will have a number of subsections or parts, indicate in the database what subsection this item will fall into.

image_x	Include a separate image field for each of the images that you will have for each item. In most cases you will not have more than four to five images of each item (and in most cases a single image). Most database/web products will allow you to reference multiple versions of an image; therefore, include in this field only the "root" name of the image. (For example, from the root file name 2001-014, you can reference the full image, named 2001-014.jpg; a thumbnail, 2001-015small.jpg; and an intermediate image, 2001-015medium.jpg.)

Example of a record output from a similar database:

Pierre Belon (1517–1564)

Les observations de plusieurs singularitez et choses memorables: Trouvées en Grece, Asie, Judée, Egypte, Arabie, et autres pays estrange [sic] (Observations of many singular and memorable things found in Greece, Asia, Judea, Egypt, Arabia, and other foreign countries)

Paris: Guillaume Cavellat, 1554

Bequest of Alexander Wetmore

By training an apothecary and botanist, Belon is also recognized by modern science as the founder of comparative anatomy and embryology in animals. He was one of the first naturalist-explorers, and his observations made this book the most thoroughly documented account of the eastern Mediterranean at the time. First published in 1553, Observations was re-printed the following year with illustrations. This woodcut accompanies the first scientific description of the giraffe, known in medieval bestiaries as the "cameleopard."

View enlarged images from this item:

Image 1

APPENDIX

E

Timeline for Contracted Online Exhibitions

Time	Event
Week 1	Concept meeting with vendor and library/archive staff: vendor receives all library/archive materials (e.g., image files or slides and script text); timetable is fleshed out.
Week 4	First design review meeting, including curators and contract staff.
Week 5	Contractor provides, at a minimum: visuals of basic concept; list for discussion of additional materials designer may need/want; mock-up of introductory page or access to an online version; suggestions as to color palette to be used.
Week 6	Second design review meeting.
Week 8	Contractor delivers final online product to library/archive in a format suitable for mounting on the library/archive website.

Dublin Core Metadata of an Online Exhibition

```
<meta name="DC.Title" content="Make the dirt fly! ; a Smithsonian Institution
       Libraries exhibition /">
<meta name="DC.Title.Alternative" content="Smithsonian Institution Libraries:
       Make the Dirt Fly!">
<meta name="DC.Title.Alternative" content="Building the Panama Canal, a
       Smithsonian Institution Libraries exhibition">
<meta name="DC.Coverage.Geog. Coded" content="ncpn ---">
<meta name="DC.Format.MIME" content="text/html">
<meta name="DC.Contributor.CorporateName" content="Smithsonian Institution.
       Libraries.">
<meta name="DC.Contributor.PersonalName" content="Kalfatovic, Martin R., 1961-">
<meta name="DC.Contributor.PersonalName" content="Danforth, Courtney.">
<meta name="DC.Publisher" content="Smithsonian Institution Libraries,">
<meta name="DC.Publisher.Place" content="Washington, D.C. :">
<meta name="DC.Date.Issued" content="1999-12-03">
<meta name="DC.Description" content="Title from title screen.">
<meta name="DC.Description.Summary" content="Electronic version of an
       exhibition to commemorate the building of the Panama Canal (1904-
       1914), the engineers and the people who accomplished the project.">
<meta name="DC.Description.Contents" content="Why build a canal? — Choosing a
       route — Making the dirt fly — Waging war on mosquitoes — Life in the
       Canal Zone — Civil engineering — An engineering icon - Did you know?
       — Suggested reading — Credits.">
<meta name="DC.Description" content="Exhibition guest curators: William E.
       Worthington, Jr. & Jeffrey K. Stine.">
<meta name="DC.Identifier.URL" content="http://www.sil.si.edu/Exhibitions/Make-
       the-Dirt-Fly/">
<meta name="DC.Language" content="english">
<meta name="DC.Subject" scheme="LCC Local" content="TC774">
<meta name="DC.Subject" scheme="Geographic" content="Panama Canal (Panama) —
       Exhibitions — Electronic information resources.">
<meta name="DC.Subject" scheme="Geographic" content="Panama Canal (Panama) —
       History — Exhibitions.">
<meta name="DC.Relation.Requires" content="Mode of access: World Wide Web. Host:
       Smithsonian Institution Libraries. URL: http://www.sil.si.edu/
       Exhibitions/Make-the-Dirt-Fly/">
```

The Katharine Kyes Leab and Daniel J. Leab American Book Prices Current Exhibition Awards

Rare Books and Manuscripts Section
Association of College and Research Libraries
American Library Association

Below are the winners and entrants in the 2001 Leab Awards.

Winners of the 2001 Leab Award

The Henry W. and Albert A. Berg Collection of English and American Literature, Humanities and Social Sciences Library, the New York Public Library

Nabokov under Glass: A Centennial Exhibition

http://www.nypl.org/research/chss/epo/nabokov

University of California, Berkeley. Water Resources Center Archives and Environmental Design Archives

Bridging the Bay: Bridging the Campus

http://www.lib.berkeley.edu/Exhibits/Bridge

List of Entrants for 2001

Alaska and Polar Regions Department, Elmer E. Rasmuson Library, University of Alaska, Fairbanks

The Butler Brothers' Gold Rush: The Nome Album, 1900–1901

http://itdc.elmer.uaf.edu/butler

Albert Gore Research Center, Middle Tennessee State University

Reflections in Time

http://janus.mtsu.edu/Reflections/index.html

Department of Special Collections, Kenneth Spencer Research Library, University of Kansas

He Who Destroyes a Good Booke, Kills Reason It Selfe

http://www.spencer.lib.ku.edu/bannedbooks.html

Exhibition Program, History of Medicine Division, National Library of Medicine

Breath of Life

http://www.nlm.nih.gov/hmd/breath/breathhome.html

History and Special Collections, Louise M. Darling Biomedical Library, University of California, Los Angeles

The Relief of Pain and Suffering

http://www.library.ucla.edu/libraries/biomed/his/PainExhibit

History and Special Collections, Louise M. Darling Biomedical Library, University of California, Los Angeles

Smallpox: Inoculation, Vaccination, Eradication

http://www.library.ucla.edu/libraries/biomed/smallpox

Information, Science and Technology Agency, British Columbia Archives

The BCC Archives Amazing Time Machine

http://www.bcarchives.gov.bc.ca/exhibits/timemach/index.htm

Manuscripts, Special Collections, University Archives Division, University of Washington Libraries

Mount Rainier National Park: 100 Years in Paradise

http://www.lib.washington.edu/exhibits/rainier

The Mark Twain Papers of the Bancroft Library, University of California, Berkeley

Mark Twain at Large: His Travels Here and Abroad

http://library.berkeley.edu/BANC/Exhibits/MTP/

Office of Research and Graduate Studies, Old Dominion University, and Old Dominion University Libraries

Old Dominion University Libraries Faculty Publications Database

http://lib.odu.edu/cgi-bin/facultypub/test1.cgi

Old Dominion University Libraries, Diehn Composers Room

From Exposition to Development: The Legacy of Composers at Hampton University

http://www.lib.odu.edu/aboutlib/musiclib/exhibits/hamptonex/onlinex.html

Old Dominion University Libraries, Diehn Composers Room

Kaleidoscope: The Musical World of Adolphus Hailstork

http://www.lib.odu.edu/aboutlib/musiclib/hailstork/index.shtml

Smithsonian Institution Libraries

Frontier Photographer: Edward S. Curtis

http://www.sil.si.edu/Exhibitions/Curtis

Smithsonian Institution Libraries

"Make the Dirt Fly!": Building the Panama Canal

http://www.sil.si.edu/Exhibitions/Make-the-Dirt-Fly

Special Collections Department, Kansas City Public Library

Frank Lauder Autochrome Collection

http://www.kclibrary.org/autochromes

Special Collections Department, Kansas City Public Library

Historical African-American Autographs from the Ramos Collection

http://www.kclibrary.org/sc/exhibits/autographs/splash.htm

Special Collections Department, University of Virginia Library

All the Hoos in Hooville: 175 Years of Life at the University of Virginia

http://www.lib.virginia.edu/exhibits/hoos

Special Collections Department, University of Virginia Library

Pop Goes the Page: Movable and Mechanical Books from the Brenda Forman Collection

http://www.lib.virginia.edu/exhibits/popup

Special Collections Department, University of Virginia Library

Red, White, Blue and Brimstone: New World Literature and the American Millennium

http://www.lib.virginia.edu/exhibits/brimstone

Special Collections Department, University of Virginia Library

Sublime Anxiety: The Gothic Family and the Outsider

http://www.lib.virginia.edu/exhibits/gothic/open.html

Special Collections, Sheridan Libraries, Johns Hopkins University

Animal, Vegetable and Mineral: Natural History Books by Ten Authors

http://naturalhistory.mse.jhu.edu

Thomas Cooper Library, University of South Carolina

Alfred Tennyson

http://www.sc.edu/library/spcoll/britlit/tenn/tenn.html

Thomas Cooper Library, University of South Carolina

Brazil: A Quincentenary Exhibit

http://www.sc.edu/library/spcoll/sccoll/brazil/brazil.html

Thomas Cooper Library, University of South Carolina

The Culture of Camellias

http://www.sc.edu/library/spcoll/nathist/camellia/camellia.html

Thomas Cooper Library, University of South Carolina

James Weldon Johnson

http://www.sc.edu/library/spcoll/amlit/johnson/johnson.html

Thomas Cooper Library, University of South Carolina

Paris Publishers of the 1920s

http://www.sc.edu/library/spcoll/amlit/paris/paris.html

Thomas Cooper Library, University of South Carolina

Trimalchio and The Great Gatsby

http://www.sc.edu/library/spcoll/amlit/trimalchio/trimalchio.html

University of North Texas Libraries, Rare Book and Texana Collections

Victorian Bookbinding: Innovation and Extravagance, 1820–1920

http://www.library.unt.edu/rarebooks/exhibits/binding

Bibliography of Exhibitions
(Gallery and Virtual)

The following bibliography consists of materials related to the creation of exhibitions. As online exhibitions are a fairly recent phenomenon, the majority of these citations are to the literature of gallery exhibitions. As many of the principles and practices of a good gallery exhibition are transferable to online exhibitions, the material will remain of interest to the online exhibition creator.

Alexander, Edward P. *Museums in Motion.* Nashville: American Association for State and Local History, 1979.

Alt, M. B. "Evaluation Didactic Exhibits: A Critical Look at Shettel's Work." *Curator* 20, no. 3 (1977): 241–258.

Alt, M. B., and K. M. Shaw. "Characteristics of Ideal Museum Exhibits." *British Journal of Psychology* 25 (1984): 25–36.

American Association of Museums, Technical Information Service. *Exhibition Planning and Management: Reprints from NAME's Recent and Recommended.* Washington, D.C.: American Association of Museums, 1992.

American Institutes for Research. Strategies for Determining Exhibit Effectiveness. Final Report Project No. V-011. Pittsburgh: American Institutes for Research, 1968.

Ames, Kenneth L., Barbara Franco, and L. Thomas Frye, eds. *Ideas and Images: Developing Interpretive History Exhibits.* Nashville: American Association for State and Local History, 1992.

Andre, Jean-Jacques. "Museum Exhibit Guidelines." *Museum Round-Up* 44 (October 1971): 30–34.

Archer, Bruce. *Systematic Method for Designers.* London: Council of Industrial Design, 1965.

The Audience in Exhibition Development. (Course Proceedings from a Training Program) Washington, D.C.: Office of Museum Programs, 1992.

Barteluk, Wendy D. M. *Library Displays on a Shoestring: 3-Dimensional Techniques for Promoting Library Services.* Metuchen, N.J.: Scarecrow, 1993.

Belcher, Michael. *Exhibitions in Museums.* Washington, D.C.: Smithsonian Institution Press, 1991.

Bell, Benjamin, Evangelia V. Dimaraki, and Mary K. Brown. "The Virtual Gallery: Exhibit Design as a Tool for Inquiry into Art, Artifact and Culture." Available at: www.tc.columbia.edu/~academic/cite/papers/edmed.EdMed.htm.

Bennington, Seddon, ed. *Handbook for Small Museums.* Perth: Western Australian Museum, 1985.

Bergman, Eugene. "Designing for Natural History." *Curator* 17, no. 3 (September 1974): 203–206.

———. "Exhibits That Flow." *Curator* 17, no. 4 (1974): 277–286.

———. "Exhibits: A Production Checklist." *Curator* 19, no. 2 (1976): 157–161.

———. "Exhibits: A Proposal for Guidelines." *Curator* 19, no. 2 (1976): 151–156.

———. "Making Exhibits: A Reference File." *Curator* 20, no. 3 (1977): 227–237.

Bitgood, Stephen C. *Knowing When Exhibit Labels Work: A Standardized Guide for Evaluating and Improving Labels.* Jacksonville, Ala.: Jacksonville State University, 1986.

Bitgood, Stephen C., Ted Finlay, and Dave Woehr. *Design and Evaluation of Exhibit Labels.* Jacksonville, Ala.: Jacksonville State University, 1986.

Blais, Andrée, ed. *Text in the Exhibition Medium.* Montreal: Société des musées québécois: Musée de la Civilisation, 1995.

Borun, M., and M. Miller. "To Label or Not to Label?" *Museum News* 58, no. 4 (1980): 64–67.

Breiteneder, Christian, Hubert Platzer, and Martin Hitz. "A Re-Usable Software Framework for Authoring and Managing Web Exhibitions." Museums and the Web 2001. Available at: www.archimuse.com/mw2001/papers/breiteneder/breiteneder2.html.

Burns, W. "A Museum Exhibition: Do-It-Yourself or Commercial?" *Curator* 12, no. 3 (1969): 160–167.

Burt, Cyril Lodowic. *Psychological Study of Typography.* Cambridge, U.K.: University Press, 1959.

Callery, Bernadette G., and Robert Thibadeau. "On Beyond Label Copy: Museum-Library Collaboration in the Development of a Smart Web Exhibit." Museums and the Web: An International Conference. 2000. Available at: www.archimuse.com/mw2000/papers/callery/callery.html.

Cameron, Duncan F. "Effective Exhibits: A Search for New Guidelines." *Museum News* 46, no. 5 (January 1968): 3–45.

Center for Museum Studies, Smithsonian Institution. *Introduction to Exhibition Design and Production, March 6–10, 1995*. Washington, D.C.: Smithsonian Institution, 1995.

———. *Introduction to Creating Museum Exhibitions, April 15–19, 1996*. Washington, D.C.: Center for Museum Studies, Smithsonian Institution, 1996.

Coen, Leigh Hayford. "The Interpretive Function in Museum Work." *Curator* 18, no. 4 (December 1975): 281–286.

Cohen-Stratyner, Barbara. "The Museum Paradox: The Co-Existence of Narrative Structure and Audience Advocacy." Master's thesis, Bank Street College of Education, 1992.

Conaway, Mary Ellen. "Exhibit Labeling: Another Alternative." *Curator* 15, no. 2 (June 1972): 161–166.

Connor, Jean. "Museum Designs Exhibition for Children." *School Arts* 69, no. 10 (1970): 28–29.

Cooper, Jonathan. "Engaging the [Museum] Visitor: Relevance, Participation and Motivation in Hypermedia Design." Available at: members.ozemail.com.au/~agjonath/museum_ed/ichim93.html.

Coplan, Kate. *Effective Library Exhibits*. Dobbs Ferry, W.Va.: Oceana, 1974.

Custerline, Gail F. "Exhibiting Archive Material: Many Faceted Manuscripts." *Museum News* 58, no. 1 (September/October 1979): 50–54.

Dana, John Cotton. *The Gloom of the Museum*. Woodstock, Vt.: Elm Tree Press, 1917.

———. *The New Museum: Selected Writings*. Woodstock, Vt.: Elm Tree Press, 1917.

———. *Should Museums Be Useful?* Newark, N.J.: The Museum, 1927.

Dandridge, F. "The Value of Design in Visual Communication." *Curator* 9, no. 4 (December 1966): 331–336.

Dean, David. *Museum Exhibition: Theory and Practice*. New York: Routledge, 1994.

Devenish, David C. "Labeling in Museum Display: A Survey and Practical Guide." *International Journal of Museum Management Curatorship* 9, no. 1 (March 1990): 63–72.

———. *Museum Display Labels: The Philosophy and Practice of Preparing Written Labels and Illustrations for Use in Museum Displays*. India: National Council of Science Museums, 1996.

Dietz, Steve. "Curating (on) the Web in an Interface Culture." 1998. Available at: www.archimuse.com/mus98/papers/dietz/dietz_curatingtheweb.html.

Dowling, Sherwood. "Incorporating an Educational Model into the Delivery of Museum Information." In Internet Society 1998 Proceedings. Available at: www.isoc.org/isoc/conferences/inet/98/proceedings/7c/7c_3.htm.

Duczmal-Pacowska, Halina. "Why Not Science Exhibitions for the Blind?" *Museum* 28, no. 3 (1976): 176–177.

Eason, Laurie P. "Evaluation of the Effectiveness of Participatory Exhibits." *Curator* 19, no. 1 (March 1976): 45–62.

Elliott, P., et al. *Studies of Visitor Behavior in Museums and Exhibitions*. Washington, D.C.: Smithsonian Institution, 1975.

Farr, Gail E. *Archives and Manuscripts, Exhibits*. Chicago: Society of American Archivists, 1980.

Franco, Barbara. "Exhibiting Archival Material: A Method of Interpretation." *Museum News* 58, no. 1 (September/October 1979): 55–59.

Frankenstein, Alfred. "Is This Exhibition Necessary?" *Museum News* 41, no. 10 (June 1963): 16–17.

Franklin, Linda Campbell. *Library Display Ideas*. Metuchen, N.J.: Scarecrow, 1989.

Gardner, George S. "The Shape of Things to Come." *Curator* 22, no. 1 (1979): 5–20.

Gifford, P. C. "Faces and Figures: A Museum/Collector Exhibition." *Curator* 8, no. 3 (September 1965): 235–247.

Gill, E. D. "Search for New Ideas on Museum Exhibits." *Curator* 10, no. 4 (December 1967): 275–278.

Glaser, Jane R., and Artemis A. Zenetou. *Museums: A Place to Work. Planning Museum Careers*. London and New York: Routledge, 1996.

Goode, George Brown. "The Museums of the Future." In *Annual Report of the Board of Regents of the Smithsonian Institution for the Year Ending June 30, 1889*, pp. 427–445. Washington, D.C.: GPO, 1891.

Goodes, Pamela A. "Traveling Exhibitions." *College and Research Libraries News* 60, no. 10 (November 1999): 835–838.

Hall, Margaret. *On Display: A Design Grammar for Museum Exhibitions*. London: Lund Humphries, 1987.

Hansen, Carl Robert. "Applying the Product Life Cycle Concept to a Temporary Exhibition in a Museum." Master's thesis, Central Michigan University, 1993.

Hatt, Robert T. "The Organization of Museum Exhibits." *Museum News* 44, no. 4 (December 1965): 17–20.

Hayes, Bartlett H., Jr. *A Study of the Relation of Museum Art Exhibitions to Education.* Washington, D.C.: Office of Education (ERDS # ED026-03), 1967.

Hayett, William. *Display and Exhibit Handbook.* New York: Reinhold, 1967.

Hirsh, Richard. "Exhibits and Installations: An Outline Guide." American Association for State and Local History Technical Leaflet No. 20. Nashville: American Association for State and Local History, 1964.

Hjorth, Jan. *How to Make a Rotten Exhibition.* Stockholm: Riksutstallningar, 1978.

Johannsen, Alice E. "Effective Exhibits from the Museum Director's Viewpoint." *Museum News* 46, no. 5 (January 1968): 38.

Jones, Walter. *Exhibit Planning, Development, and Implementation Procedures.* Jacksonville, Ala.: Jacksonville State University, 1986.

Jones, William K. "The Exhibit of Documents: Preparation, Matting, and Display Techniques." American Association for State and Local History Technical Leaflet No. 75. Nashville: American Association for State and Local History, 1974.

Kalfatovic, Martin R. "Online with the Show." *Library Journal NetConnect* (Winter 2001): 32–35.

Karp, Ivan, and Steven D. Lavine, eds. *Exhibiting Cultures: The Poetics and Politics of Museum Display.* Washington, D.C.: Smithsonian Institution Press, 1991.

Kjeldsberg, Peter Andreas. "A New Permanent Exhibition at Ringve Museum, Trondheim." *CIMCIM Newsletter* 9 (1981): 35–37.

Klein, Larry. *Exhibits: Planning and Design.* New York: Madison Square, 1986.

Leavitt, Thomas W. "Meaning in Exhibition Programs." *Museum News* 42, no. 6 (February 1964): 17–19.

———. "The Need for Critical Standards in History Museum Exhibits: A Case in Point." *Curator* 10, no. 2 (June 1967): 91–94.

———. "Curators, Collections and Exhibits." *Museum News* 46, no. 10 (June 1968): 32–34.

Linn, Marcia C. "Exhibit Evaluation: Informed Decision Making. *Curator* 19, no. 4 (December 1976): 292–302.

Loomis, R. J. *Museum Visitor Evaluation: New Tool for Museum Management.* Nashville: American Association for State and Local History, 1987.

Lowry, M. W. *Planning Educational Exhibits.* Athens, Ga.: n.p., 1930.

Martin, David. "Working with Designers. 1. Getting Started." *Museums Journal* 90, no. 4 (April 1990): 31–38.

Marty, Paul F. "On-Line Exhibit Design: The Socio-technological Impact of Building a Museum over the World Wide Web." *Journal of the American Society for Information Science* 51, no. 1 (2000): 24–32.

McKay, Tom. "Exhibiting Local History." *Museum News* 55, no. 3 (January/February 1977): 35–36.

McLean, Fiona. *Marketing the Museum.* New York: Routledge, 1997.

McManus, P. "Oh Yes, They Do: How Museum Visitors Read Labels and Interact with Exhibit Texts." *Curator* 32, no. 3 (1989): 174–189.

———. "Watch Your Language! People Do Read Labels." *ILVS Review: A Journal of Visitor Behavior* 1, no. 2 (1990): 125–127.

Milekic, Slavko. "Designing Digital Environments for Art Education/Exploration." *Journal of the American Society for Information Science* 51, no. 1 (2000): 49–56.

Miles, Roger S. *The Design of Educational Exhibits.* 2nd ed. London and Boston: Unwin Hyman, 1988.

Miller, Leon Gordon. "The Industrial Designer: New Member of the Museum Team." *Curator* 6, no. 2 (1968): 187–190.

Milnes, Colin. "A Designer's Aspect." *Museums Journal* 82, no. 1 (1982): 44–46.

Moore, George. "Displays for the Sightless." *Curator* 11, no. 4 (December 1968): 292–296.

Neal, Arminta. *Exhibits for the Small Museum.* Nashville: American Association for State and Local History, 1976.

———. *Gallery and Case Design.* Nashville: American Association for State and Local History, 1980. Slides, sound cassette, and script.

Neustupny, Jiri. "The Educational Value of Labels." *Museum* 1, no. 3–4 (December 1948): 162–163.

Nicol, E. *The Development of Validated Museum Exhibits.* Washington, D.C.: U.S. Department of Health, Education, and Welfare, 1969.

Nowack, Jeannine. *Building a Portable Table Top Exhibit.* Avon, N.Y.: Western New York Association of Historical Agencies, 1989.

Oberlander, Jon, et al. "Exploring a Gallery with Intelligent Labels." In *Museum Interactive Multimedia 1997: Cultural Heritage Systems Design and Interfaces: Selected Papers from ICHIM 97, the Fourth International Conference on Hypermedia and Interactivity in Museums, Paris, France, 3–5*

September 1997, ed. David Bearman and Jennifer Trant, pp. 80–87. Pittsburgh: Archives and Museum Informatics, 1997.

One Hundred and One Ideas from History News. Nashville: American Association for State and Local History, 1975.

Paolini, Paolo, Thimoty Barbieri, Paolo Loiudice, Francesca Alonzo, Marco Zanti, and Giuliano Gaia. "Visiting a Museum Together: How to Share a Visit to a Virtual World." *Journal of the American Society for Information Science* 51, no. 1 (2000): 33–38.

Parr, Albert E. "Designed for Display." *Curator* 2, no. 4 (1959): 333–334.

———. *Mostly about Museums.* New York: American Museum of Natural History, 1959.

———. "Patterns of Progress in Exhibition." *Curator* 5, no. 4 (1962): 329–345.

———. "Realism and Romanticism in Museum Exhibits." *Curator* 6, no. 2 (1963): 174–185.

———. "Remarks on Layout, Display, and Response to Design." *Curator* 7, no. 2 (1964): 131–142.

Peart, Bob. "Impact of Exhibit Type on Knowledge Gain, Attitudes, and Behavior." *Curator* 27, no. 3 (1984): 220–237.

Pierroux, Palmyre. "Art in Networks: Information and Communication Technology in Art Museums." Available at: www.media.uio.no/internettiendring/publikasjoner/tekst/Pierroux/02Contents.html.

Pizer, Laurence. "How Not to Cooperate: A Co-Sponsored Exhibit Ends in Confusion." *History News* 35, no. 10 (October 1980): 7–10.

Rare Book and Manuscript Section, ACRL. "Library Web Exhibitions." Available at: www.library.yale.edu/~mtheroux/webecac.htm.

Robertson, John C. "Maps in a Museum." *Museum Round-Up* 50 (April 1973): 24–27.

"The Role of the Designer in the Museum." *Museums Journal* 70, no. 2 (1970): 63–68.

Routzahn, Evart Grant, and Mary Swain Routzahn. *The ABC of Exhibit Planning.* New York: Russell Sage Foundation, 1918.

Salpeter, Bob. "How Nonscientists Design a Highly Scientific Exhibit." *Curator* 18, no. 2 (June 1975): 130–139.

Schnaeffer, B. "Exhibits and Ideas." *Curator* 1, no. 2 (1958): 25–33.

Schudles, W. K. F. "Basic Principles of Exhibit Design." *Curator* 10, no. 1 (1967): 49–53.

Screven, Chandler G. *The Measurement and Facilitation of Learning in the Museum Environment: An Experimental Analysis.* Washington, D.C.: Smithsonian Institution Press, 1974.

———. "The Effectiveness of Guidance Devices on Visitor Learning." *Curator* 18, no. 3 (1975): 219–243.

———. "Exhibit Evaluation: A Goal-Referenced Approach." *Curator* 19, no. 4 (December 1976): 271–290.

———. "Museums and Informal Education." *CMS Bulletin* 1, no. 1 (May 1993). Available at: http://museumstudies.si.edu/bull/may93/screven.htm.

Serrell, Beverly. *Making Exhibit Labels: A Step-by-Step Guide.* Nashville: American Association for State and Local History, 1982.

———. *Exhibit Labels: An Interpretive Approach.* Walnut Creek, Calif.: Alta Mira, 1996.

Shettel, H. "Exhibits: Art Form or Educational Medium?" *Museum News* 52 (1993): 32–41.

———. *Paying Attention: Visitors and Museum Exhibitions.* Washington, D.C.: American Association of Museums, 1998.

Silver, David. "Interfacing American Culture: The Perils and Potentials of Virtual Exhibitions." *American Quarterly* 49, no. 4 (1997): 825–850.

Sorsby, B. D., and S. D. Horne. "The Readability of Museum Labels." *Museums Journal* 80, no. 3 (1980): 157–159.

Stansfield, Geoff. "Nature on Display: Trends in Natural History Museum Exhibitions." *Museums Journal* 86, no. 2 (1986): 97–103.

Szemere, Ádám, ed. *The Problems of Contents, Didactics, and Esthetics of Modern Museum Exhibitions.* Budapest: István Éri, 1978.

Taylor, Samuel, ed. *Try It! Improving Exhibits through Formative Evaluation.* Washington, D.C.: Association of Science-Technology Centers, 1991.

Thomas, Wendy, and Danielle Boily. "Virtual Exhibition Production: A Reference Guide." Museums and the Web: An International Conference. 1998. Available at: www.archimuse.com/mw98/papers/boily/boily_paper.html.

UNESCO. *Temporary and Travelling Exhibitions.* Paris: ICOM, 1963.

Velarde, Giles. *Designing Exhibitions.* London: Design Council, 1988.

Visitor Studies Conference. *Visitor Studies: Theory, Research, and Practice.* 6 vols. Collected papers from the annual Visitor Studies Conference. Jacksonville, Ala.: Visitor Studies Association, 1988–1993.

Walsh, Peter. "The Neon Paintbrush: Seeing, Technology, and the Museum as Metaphor." *Journal of the American Society for Information Science* 51, no. 1 (2000): 39–48.

Warren, Jefferson T. *Exhibit Methods.* New York: Sterling, 1972.

INDEX

A

Access
Americans with Disabilities Act
compliance and, 21
design of exhibition pages and,
67–69
online guides for, 68, 70–71
to online library collections, 2
Active Server Pages (ASP), 66
websites for, 69
Administration exhibition policies,
21–22
Adobe Acrobat PDF (Portable
Document Format), 68
Aesthetic exhibitions, 3–4
American Museum of Natural History
(New York), 2
*American Treasures of the Library of
Congress,* 13–14, 17
Americans with Disabilities Act (ADA),
21, 68
"Amphibian Species of the World," 2
Anniversaries as idea sources, 10–11
Archer, Bruce, 73–74
Archival collections online, 2
Halifax and Its People / 1749–1999,
89–90
Lee Wilson and Company Archives, 90
Utah's Road to Statehood, 89–90
Archive director, 39–40
Audience, 22
Awards, 92–94, 109–110

B

Belcher, Michael, 16
*Bibliotheca Canadiana. A Historical
Survey of Canadian Bibliography /
Étude Historique de la Bibliographie
Canadienne,* 88–89
Birds!, 88–89
Boily, Danielle, 35
Braille readers, 57
Bridging the Bay: Bridging the Campus,
92
Budget proposal, 23

C

*California Pacific Exposition: San Diego
1935–1936,* 12, 17

Cameras, 44–45
Canada at Scale: Maps of Our History,
11–12, 17
Captions. *See* Labels/captions
*Capture of Fort William and Mary, New
Castle, New Hampshire, The,* 11, 17
*Cartographic Creation of New England,
The,* 11, 17
Cascading style sheets (CSS), 55–58,
61–62
Celebrating the Boar, 14, 17
Chicago Fire, The, 11, 17
*Children's Books of the Early Soviet Era:
Yesterday, Today and . . . Tomorrow,*
12, 17
Churchill: The Evidence, 12, 17
Cold Fusion (Allaire), 66
websites for, 70
Color and design, 75, 77–80
Common Gateway Interface (CGI)
scripting, 63–64, 68–69
*Common Wealth, The: Treasures from the
Collections of the Library of
Virginia,* 13, 17
Connies, 12, 17
Conservator, 41
Consultants, 41–42
Content management, 21–22
Contracted exhibition design, 85, 107
Copyright/credit, 30–32, 36, 103–104
Credit. *See* Copyright/credit
Curator
exhibition policies and, 22
roles/responsibilities, 40
Curtis, George W., 98

D

*Damned Art, The: An Exhibition of
Books Relating to the History of
Witchcraft and Demonology,* 92
Databases
for online exhibitions, 65–67
sample structure for, 105–106
websites for, 69
*Daughter of Earth: Agnes Smedley and
Smedley-MacKinnon Collections,*
24, 37
Deconstructing Web Graphics, 51
Decorative fonts. *See* Fonts

Descriptions. *See* Copyright/credit;
Labels/captions
Design
color and, 75, 77–80
contracting work for, 85
for databases, 66
exhibition proposal and, 23
fonts, 80–82
labels and, 82–83
metadata and, 85–86
navigation principles and, 83–85
process of, 74
quick tips for, 86
roles/responsibilities of designer,
40–41
screen layout and, 74–77
websites for, 87
Designing Web Graphics.3, 51
Didactic exhibitions, 3, 5–6
Digital Collections Inventory Report, 1
Digital collections versus online exhibitions, 1–6
Digital Scriptorium, 2
Digitizing
Do You Remember, When, 90–91
*Edible Monument, The: The Art of
Food for Festivals,* 90–91
file formats for saving images, 48–51
methods of, 44–45
preservation and, 51–52
standards for, 46–48
use of text images, 83
*Writing on Hands: Memory and
Knowledge in Early Modern
Europe,* 91
Dino at the Sands, 14–15, 17
Director of library. *See* Administration
Display fonts. *See* Fonts
Do You Remember, When, 90–91
Document type definition (DTD),
58–59
*Dr. Charles Wolf Collection of Irish
Postage Stamps, The,* 11, 17
*Dr. Seuss Went to War: A Catalog of
Political Cartoons by Dr. Seuss,* 12,
18
Duane Hanson: An Exhibition, 3–4, 7
Dublin Core, 85, 108
Dynamic HTML (DHTML), 55, 61

E

Early American Fiction project, 2
Earth and the Heavens, The: The Art of the Mapmaker, 11, 18
Edible Monument, The: The Art of Food for Festivals, 90–91
Editorial position
    exhibition policies and, 22
    roles/responsibilities, 41
Education consultant, 41–42
Emotive exhibitions, 3–4
Enduring Legacy of Paper Bindings, The, 12, 18
Entertaining exhibitions, 3, 6
Environment. *See* Work environment
Evocative exhibitions, 3, 5
Exhibition policies, 21
Exhibition proposal, 22–23
Exhibitions. *See also* Online exhibitions
    historical aspects of, 16
    organization of site and, 24–26
Exhibitions in Museums, 16
Exhibitions officer, 21
Exploring Africa: An Exhibit of Maps and Travel Narratives, 11, 18
Extensibility of XML, 58
eXtensible HyperText Markup Language (XHTML), 60–62
eXtensible Markup Language (XML), 58–59, 62

F

File transfer, 48
Filemaker Pro, 66, 70
Fonts, 80–82
1492: An Ongoing Voyage, 11, 18
From Alchemy to Chemistry: Five Hundred Years of Rare and Interesting Books, 89
From Exposition to Development: The Legacy of Composers at Hampton University, 14, 18
From Smithson to Smithsonian, 10, 18, 32, 37
Frontier Photographer: Edward S. Curtis, 26, 37, 100–102
Frontiers, Frontières, Fronteras: René Derouin, 31, 37
Fruits of a Research Collection, 14, 18

G

Galleries. *See also specific sites*
    bibliography of exhibitions, 111–114
    navigation principles and, 84
    policies of, 21–22
    retrospective conversions and, 72–73
Gallery of Bloomsday Cards, A, 6–7

Girls Fight for a Living, 12, 18
Graphical Interchange Format (GIF), 48–49, 52
Graphical User Interface (GUI), 55
Great Assemblage, A: An Exhibit of Judaica, 27–28, 37
Gutenberg Bible, 2–3

H

Halifax and Its People / 1749–1999, 89–90
Handbook for Digital Projects: A Management Tool for Preservation and Access, 52
Harley L. McDevitt Collection on the Spanish Inquisition, 25
Highlights of the Map Collection, National Library of Scotland, 11, 18
Historical aspects of exhibitions, 16
History of Railway Photography, The, 12, 18
History of the Houston Public Library, 14, 18
Hjorth, Jan, 35
How to Make a Rotten Exhibition, 35
Hyperlinks, 85
HyperText Markup Language (HTML)
    as basic web language, 54–55
    contracting work and, 85
    web/database interfaces and, 66–67
    XML/XHTML and, 59–60
HyperText Transfer Protocol (HTTP), 55, 63

I

Idea sources, 9–16
Image compression. *See* Digitizing
Images. *See* Digitizing
Intellectual property issues, 36
International Standards Organization (ISO), 54
Irish Treasures from the O'Hegarty Irish Collection, 18

J

Jackie Gleason Collection, The, 14, 19
Java, 65
JavaScript, 64–65, 69
John Bull and Uncle Sam: Four Centuries of British-American Relations, 31, 37
Joint Photographic Experts Group (JPEG), 48–50, 53

K

Keeping Our Word: Preserving Information across the Ages, 14, 19
Kodak Photo CD (PCD), 49

L

Labels/captions, 29–36, 82–83
Leab *American Book Prices* Current Exhibition Awards, 92, 109–110
Lee Wilson and Company Archives, 90
Library collections online, 2–3
Library director, 39–40

M

Maintenance and exhibition proposal, 23
"Make the Dirt Fly!" 30–31, 38
"Making of America," 2
Management and exhibition policies, 21–22
Many Talents of John Gorham Palfrey, Our First Dean, The, 32, 38
Markup languages
    elements of style and, 56–57
    types of, 54–56, 58–61
McClung, Patricia A., 1
Metadata, 85–86, 108
Morris Udall: A Lifetime of Service to Arizona and the United States, 5, 7
Multimedia, 51, 53. *See also* Digitizing
Museum collections online, 2, 92–94

N

Nabokov under Glass: A Centennial Exhibition, 92–93
Narrative. *See* Script
National Portrait Gallery of the Smithsonian Institution, 2, 8
National Portrait Gallery of the Smithsonian Institution, 7
Nazi Olympics, The: Berlin 1936, 4
Night before Christmas by Clement C. Moore, Illustrated, The 12–13, 19
Nile Notes of a Howadji: American Travelers in Egypt, 1837 to 1901, 98–99
1997: A Year of Many Anniversaries, 11, 19
Nos Los Inquisidores, 25, 38
Notable events as idea sources, 11
Notre Dame v. USC Game, The: 22 October 1977, 6–7

O

Object caption, 30
Object list
    exhibition proposal and, 23–24
    selection/preparation, 26–29
OCLC, Inc., 2
Odd/unusual as idea sources, 15–16
Online Exhibit of Erotica, An, 5, 7
Online exhibitions
    bibliography of exhibitions, 111–114

navigation principles of, 83–85
types of, 3–6
versus digital collections, 1–6
versus gallery exhibitions, 34–35, 73
websites of, 94–95
Online Medieval and Classical
Library, 2–3
Organization of site, 24–26
*Out of This World: Canadian Science
Fiction and Fantasy,* 31, 38
Oveta Culp Hobby, the Little Colonel, 25,
38

P

Page layout. *See* Design; Markup languages
Palettes. *See* Color and design
*Paper Dinosaurs, 1824–1969: An
Exhibition of Original Publications
from the Collections of the Linda
Hall Library,* 6–7
*Past Perfect: The Jewish Experience in
Early-Twentieth-Century Postcards,*
5, 7
Photoshop file format (PSD), 49
PHP, 66, 70
Portable Network Graphics (PNG), 49,
53
Postcards
Gallery of Bloomsday Cards, A, 6
*Past Perfect: The Jewish Experience
in Early-Twentieth-Century
Postcards,* 5
Powers of Persuasion, 5, 7
*Printmaker's Journey: The Graphic Art of
Jorg Schmeisser,* 3, 7
Production staff, 42
Programming
Common Gateway Interface
(CGI) scripting, 63–64
JavaScript and, 64–65
Project Jumbo, 6–7
Proposals (sample), 98–99
Pull quotes, 30

R

Rare Book and Manuscripts Section
(RBMS) Awards, 92, 109–110
*Recent Acquisitions in NCSU Libraries'
Special Collections, 1998–1999,*
24, 38
Reflections in Time, 38
Relief of Pain and Suffering, 4, 7
Research Libraries Information
Network (RLIN), 2
Retrospective conversions
*Damned Art, The: An Exhibition of
Books Relating to the History of
Witchcraft and Demonology,* 92

galleries and, 72–73
Science and the Artist's Book, 92
*Women's Bodies, Women's Property:
Limited Ownership under the
Law: German Common-Law
Books Illustrated in the
Fourteenth Century,* 91–92
*Romanovs, The: Their Empire, Their
Books. The Political, Religious,
Cultural, and Social Life of Russia's
Imperial House,* 29, 38
*Rum, Riot, and Reform: Maine and the
History of American Drinking,* 30, 38

S

Sans serif fonts. *See* Fonts
Scanners, 44–45
Science and the Artist's Book, 25, 38, 92
Screen layout, 74–77
Script, 29–36, 64–65, 100–102
Sculpture of Donal Hord, The, 3, 7
*Season's Greetings: Holiday Cards from
the Archives of American Art,* 4, 7
Security
Common Gateway Interface (CGI)
scripting and, 64
JavaScript and, 65
Selection and gallery policies, 21
Serif fonts. *See* Fonts
Sitts, Maxine K., 52
Special collections as idea sources,
11–12
Specific materials as idea sources,
11–12
Speech-synthesis tool, 57
Staff
exhibition proposal and, 23
roles/responsibilities, 39–43
Standard Generalized Markup
Language (SGML), 54, 61
Statement of authorship (responsibility), 32
Style sheets. *See* Markup languages
fonts and, 82
*Sublime Anxiety: The Gothic Family and
the Outsider,* 5, 8
Systematic Method for Designers, 73–74

T

Tag Image File Format (TIFF), 49–50,
52–53
Teams. *See* Staff
Technical staff, 41
Tempus Fugit: Time Flies, 94
Themes as idea sources, 12–13
*They Still Draw Pictures: Drawings
Made by Spanish Children during
the Spanish Civil War,* 4, 8
Thomas, Wendy, 35

Timelines, 23
*Travel Photographs from the Collections
of the Ohio Historical Society,* 5, 8
Treasures as idea sources, 13–15
*Treasures from Europe's National
Libraries,* 13, 19
*Treasures from the O'Hegarty Irish
Collection,* 13
*Treasures of Florida Libraries: A
Celebration of Rare and Unique
Materials,* 13, 19
Treasures of the APS, 13, 19
Treasures of the Royal Library, 13, 19
*219 Loyola: Building a Library for New
Orleans,* 11, 19
Typeface, 80

U

Use policies. *See* Copyright
User agent, 57–58
Utah's Road to Statehood, 89–90

V

Validation of XML, 58
"Virtual Exhibition Production: A
Reference Guide," 35
Virtual Reality Modeling Language
(VRML), 68
*Voyages: A Smithsonian Libraries
Exhibition,* 76–77

W

*Walt Whitman and the Development of
"Leaves of Grass,"* 27, 38
Web/database interfaces, 66–67
Web-deliverable images, 50–51
Weinman, Lynda, 51
*Women's Bodies, Women's Property:
Limited Ownership under the Law:
German Common-Law Books
Illustrated in the Fourteenth
Century,* 91–92
Work done as idea sources, 15
Work environment
integration of online exhibit into,
43
online exhibition and, 34–36
World Wide Web Consortium (W3C),
56, 58
WorldCat, 2
*Writing on Hands: Memory and
Knowledge in Early Modern Europe,*
91
Writings of Paul Laurence Dunbar, The,
27, 38

X

XHTML, 54
contracting work and, 85

Martin R. Kalfatovic is the Digital Projects Librarian and Head of the New Media Office at Smithsonian Institution Libraries, where he overseas the digitizing efforts of the Libraries. These efforts include online exhibitions and digital editions and collections. An active member of the Library Information and Technology Association, he is a former editor of the *Library and Information Technology (LITA) Newsletter* (1997 to 2000) and was named LITA web coordinator for 2000 to 2002. He is a frequent contributor of articles and reviews to various publications. He is also an adjunct faculty member at the Catholic University of America's School of Library and Information Science, where he teaches library automation and museum librarianship.